A NEW PEOPLE OF GOD

OF GOD

A Study in Salvationism

The Cover has been inspired by this dramatic expression in *The Officer* of 1893 in an article on the work of officers.

"Our work...to create a *new* people for God out of the raw material around us." Like Ezekiel our Army is to come "...from the dead."

"...dead in sin, dead to their highest interests, dead to God's claims dead to the dangers of eternity without God;..."

"To definitely get a sinner converted and enrolled and in fighting form, is a greater victory than putting a dozen people on the rolls, who are members of churches and missions,..."

"*Go for the dead,* and out of those ranks create a force who shall stand for God."

"Nothing calls attention in the house so much as the new baby."

A NEW PEOPLE OF GOD, A Study in Salvationism

© 1984 by John Rosario Rhemick
All Rights Reserved
Published by The Salvation Army
10 W. Algonquin Road, Des Plaines, Illinois 60016

First Printing, 1993
Printed in the United States of America

Library of Congress Catalog Card Number: 93-93513
ISBN: 1-883719-00-3

Table of Contents

Dedication

To my dearest wife, Pat, without whose constant support, encouragement, and selfless labor, none of this would have been possible, and to my dear children, Kathleen, Heather, and Kelly, all of whom lived through the trying times of this educational endeavor. Often they were deprived of quality time with dad. I love these people with all my heart, especially for their understanding.

About the Author

John Rhemick was born in Rome, New York on August 1, 1939. While in high school he received a music scholarship to Valley Forge Military Academy and graduated in 1957. His college education began at Valley Forge in 1958 continued at Utica College of Syracuse University in 1959 after which he entered The Salvation Army School for Officers' Training in the Eastern Territory in September of 1959.

Commissioned and ordained as a minister in The Salvation Army in June of 1960, John served as an officer for seven years. He studied at The New York State University at Buffalo, Bryant Stratton Business Institute in Buffalo, and Columbia University in New York City. During this time he served in corps, divisional, and territorial appointments. He also served as the first director of The Salvation Army's Greenwich Village Project ministering to diverse groups of people in the drug and rock cultures of that generation and place.

John married Patricia Grace Harding from Windsor, Ontario, Canada in June of 1967 and became the Director of Development for the New York Bible Society (now the International Bible Society).

In 1970 he entered Asbury College where he completed his undergraduate degree majoring in psychology while serving as Development Officer with the college and a United Methodist Pastor. He continued his studies at Asbury Theological Seminary where he received his M. Div. in 1973. He then moved with his wife and daughter to Chicago where he attended Northwestern University receiving his MA in Religious and Theological Studies in 1975 and his Ph.D. in 1984.

Reinstated as an officer with the commissioning of his wife in June of 1976, they were appointed to East Chicago, IN as corps officers. John has 17 years of pastoral experience, has recently served as the Director of Curriculum at The Salvation Army School for Officers' Training and has been the Education Secretary for the Central Territory for the last six years.

As Education Secretary John has been instrumental in developing a holy land study program for officers, a training program for Auxiliary Officers, an officer continuing education program with undergraduate and graduate degree possibilities, and a territorial School of Ministry program for laymen as well as officers, also offering undergraduate and graduate degree programs. His department also administers an education assistance program for officers, a territorial student loan program for salvationists, and an officer's child scholarship program for children of officers.

A member of Phi Theta Kappa Junior College Honor Society and the Wesleyan Theological Society, John was honored by being included in Who's Who in American Christian Leadership in 1989. He currently resides in Oak Park with his wife Patricia, and two of his three daughters, Heather and Kelly. His oldest daughter, Kathleen, lives in Columbia Missouri where she works and is attending The University of Missouri at Columbia.

Preface

The Salvation Army was the only major religious organization to evolve during the flurry of Church activity directed toward the poor of Victorian England. While a social and charitable organization, it was first and foremost an evangelical Christian movement. As such, its theology would be expected to have played an important role in its establishment as a religious denomination, international in scope. However, with the exception of a few papers on the theology of William Booth, its founder, the theology of The Salvation Army has received little attention. This paper is concerned with the theology of the Army and its role in the Army's successful formation.

Victorian culture was investigated in relation to the poor classes upon whom the Army focused its attention. Literature written by the Army and by those outside the movement was considered to determine the important theological emphases of the Army in its formative years and their significance in establishing the Army.

Victorian culture was dominated by a word emphasis embodied within middle-class values and sanctions. In important respects the lower classes were more closely related to the image culture of past generations. The poor found themselves excluded from the opportunities and benefits of Victorian life. Disfranchised, they neither belonged to their world nor had much hope for a brighter future.

The theology of the Army, while evangelical in character and particularly Methodistic in doctrinal formulation, presented a theology of salvation, not alone in narrow terms of sins forgiven but as a way to live. This theology of salvation was the very life of the Army. The doctrines of salvation and sanctification answered the disfranchisement of the poor. To the many who felt isolated, their content conveyed a sense of belonging and the dramatic expression of this content inspired a present as well as an eternal hope.

The theology of The Salvation Army in its formative years, both in its doctrinal formulations and in the nature of its expression was largely responsible for its successful establishment as a major religious denomination of a most peculiar type. Organized along military lines, it understood itself more as a new people of God, somewhat in the spirit of the Israelites of old.

Chapter I
Introduction

This study will examine the theology of The Salvation Army in its formative years and its primary importance in the Army's development as a religious and social movement. Theological expression as well as doctrinal formulations are considered in the social and cultural context of Victorian England. This study will establish three positions with regard to the theology of The Salvation Army in its formative years: (1) that Salvation Army theology is a direct derivative of Methodist theological thought; (2) that the essence of the Army's theological constructs, namely its doctrines on salvation and sanctification, and its unwritten doctrine of the Church, met a critical social and cultural need, namely the disfranchisement of the masses of poor people from societal provisions and possibilities; (3) that the nature of the Army's theological expression also met a critical social and cultural need, namely the deprivation of feeling and faith, the emotive side of human nature, within the lives of the disfranchised.

The importance of this study lies first in the supposition that it is integrally related to one of the perennial theological problems of the Christian Church: how is the Church to combine faith and works in such a way as to treat the salvation of the soul with ultimate concern while not forsaking the equally demanding obligation of the Church to care for the physical well-being of the poor and destitute. The Salvation Army was able to bring the two concerns together in a most effective way. It was called into being to save the masses of humanity lost in sin. As an expression of this task of evangelism, a program of social concern was envisioned and enacted which offered practical assistance for critical survival needs.

Secondly, the questions about the Army's successful beginning and the causes of that success bring into focus a role model for the Church mission today as the Church continues to be concerned about the masses of unchurched and needy people throughout the world. However, The Salvation Army itself is particularly in need of this investigation because it is experiencing somewhat of an identity problem. Has the Army become what it was intended to be? Is it true to its beginnings? What in the past is important for today, and what should be abandoned? This investigation provides a backdrop against which fundamental questions like these can be studied and discussed. What the Army was and why it became so has a bearing on what it is and what it will be. Without an adequate self-understanding, the Army will be pushed in all directions by all kinds of strange winds rather than steering its own course through the storms that face it. This study is one effort toward the formulation of that adequate self-understanding.

Even more weight is added to this study when one discovers that very little of this kind of introspection and investigative effort has been done, and no effort has been made at a critical understanding of the Army's formative years with respect to its theology. Army literature in its formative years was quite substantial. In addition to the weekly mission magazine which became *The War Cry*, the Army began to publish *All the World*, a report on its overseas work, and *The*

Officer, a magazine of information, instruction, and inspiration for the commissioned officers (ordained clergy) of the Army. For a short time *The Darkest England Gazette* was published reporting on the newly formed Salvation Army Social Wing and its special work among the poor. Many books were written in these early years such as *Salvation Mine* (1881), *The Coming Army* (1888), and *Heathen England* (1891). Hundreds of newspaper and magazine articles were written by the Army.

As one might expect of a new movement fighting for credibility and acceptance, this literature was inspirational and apologetic. Most writings were historical in nature reporting on the work being done. In everything that the Army published or presented for publication, the Army affirmed its divine origin or its effectiveness or the appropriateness of its methods, and in many cases included all of these concerns and more. Here was proclamation rather than introspective self-examination. The Salvation Army was no doubt too young, too busy, and too successful to ask questions about itself. However, after a century of existence this Christian movement has arrived at the point in time when these kinds of questions should be raised. A first step in this process is a critical understanding of the Army's effective beginnings.

This study argues that the theology of the Army played a vital role in its successful establishment as a religious and social institution with international appeal. While the preeminence of things spiritual cannot be missed by anyone seriously considering The Salvation Army, that theology has received very little critical consideration. With the exception of the doctrine book and a very short book authored by Commissioner Alfred G. Cunningham (also bearing the name of the Founder, General William Booth), *The Bible: Its Divine Revelation, Inspiration and Authority*, no Army literary works have been written on the subject of Army theology or its relationship to the Army's successful establishment. There were valid reasons for this in the Army's formative years.

The Salvation Army was born in a time when a cold intellectualism was pervading many of the churches of England. Verbose orations from the pulpit were the order of the day for many houses of worship. By the late Victorian period criticism of this practice was growing, and the Army consciously opposed this practice as inappropriate to save the lost masses from their sins. There was no time to talk about fine points of doctrine while millions were dying and going to hell. They needed to hear the simple story that Jesus died to save sinners, that all were sinners who needed that salvation, and that sinners could avail themselves of the mercy and grace of God. While this was straightforward evangelical theology, it was couched not in contemplative discourse but in fervent proclamation. Today, however, contemplative discourse in terms of a critical investigation of the Army's theology is called for because, while asserting vehemently that its work is religious and spiritual, Army literature still has little to do with thinking and arguing theology.

In recent years the major literary work published by The Salvation Army has been a multivolume work, *The History of The Salvation Army*. The first volume was written by Robert Sandall and published in 1947. The sixth volume was written by Frederick Coutts and published in 1973. Any theological implications have to be dug out from the historical material which is, of course, primary. The same is true of early accounts of history such as is found in St. John Ervine's biography of William Booth, *God's Soldier*, or George Scott Railton's book *Heathen England* which gives a history of the first twenty-five years of The Salvation Army. While Army theology is more directly discussed in books like Catherine Booth's *Personal Christianity* and *Aggressive Christianity*, it is not dealt with in any critical sense. These are works that present a personal God for the individual and how the individual is to live out his Christian experience. Here are proclamations of what the Army believes but no presentation of Army theology for people to consider as theology, much less the more important question of its value to the movement.

In William Booth's most famous book *Darkest England and the Way Out*, a scheme for dealing with the problem of poverty and degradation in the United Kingdom is proposed. Again, theological concerns of the Army may be sifted out, but this kind of study is not germane to the intent of the book. While there have been theses written on certain aspects of theology such as the theology of William Booth, to my knowledge none of them deals with the fundamental question of this study; the question of the significance of Army theology in the establishment of the Army as a valid and lasting denomination.

Many regard Salvation Army theology as a simple derivative of Methodism, and assume that this is the last word to be said on the subject. Regarding this research, some have asked what there was about Army theology that required special attention. Simply put, this study argues that Army theology, and especially the expression of that theology, played the major role in establishing the Army as a religious and social institution, not only in England but also around the world.

This study will show that theologically The Salvation Army is a derivative of Methodism particularly, but that more than a simple preaching of this theology, carried directly to the poor, was the significant cause of the Army's success in becoming a new religious order. It was in meeting cultural and social needs that the Army won a listening ear from the poor and working class and eventually earned a place in the hearts of many of them.

In this study two culturally inculcated perceptions of life are identified. While these two perceptions of life in which the seeds of this new denomination were nurtured existed together, it was the domination of the one over the other which gave rise to these needs. The Army satisfied these needs for a significant number of disfranchised people. Its dramatic expression of theology became a vehicle by which new symbols of theological import were substituted for those considered to be ineffective in reaching out to the unchurched masses. While there was a familiarity with the theological constructs of Victorian society which bred contempt among the poor of England, the dramatic expression of those constructs captured the imagination of a significant segment of this alienated class at home and in other countries around the world. Among these people, the dramatic expression of the Army's theological constructs, which are called "Grand Ideas" in the study, culminated in a consciousness of individual worth no matter how sinful or destitute one might be and, even more, the value of every individual to God.

Part I

The Beginning

Chapter II

The Salvation Army, Its Founders, and Founding

William Booth and Catherine Mumford Booth were both born in 1829: William in Nottingham on April 10, 1829, and Catherine in Ashbourne, Derbyshire, on January 17, 1829. While William is recognized as the indisputable founder of The Salvation Army, his wife, Catherine, was totally involved in his ministry from the beginning, before the Army, and second only to him as a founding inspiration for this new religious and social movement.

William Booth grew up, the only son of the family, with an elder sister, Ann, and two younger sisters, Emma and Mary. His parents, Samuel and Mary (Moss) Booth, were poor people when they moved to Nottingham, so the children grew up in humble surroundings in close contact with the noise and crowding of industrialism. At six years of age William had the opportunity to enroll in school under a Mr. Biddulph. According to Begbie, one of the most respected biographers of William Booth, Booth had little commendation for this school.[1] Attending the local parish church at this time, Booth also found little religious stimulation, either in the church or in his own home. However, Begbie points out that still Booth possessed a keen conviction of the existence of God. He writes:

> "One thing is certain. Throughout his childhood William
> Booth was overshadowed by a feeling of the nearness of God.
> He never knew the isolation of even a transitory atheism.
> Whether he was mischievous or good, whether he was
> 'worldly' or unselfish, he believed in God.[2]

No doubt due to sparse family resources and the quality
of family relationships, William's childhood was not happy.
But Begbie and a later historian, Robert Sandall, found in
Booth's early childhood, experiences that would prepare
him for his crowning work as founder and international
leader of The Salvation Army. On this Begbie quotes Booth
himself but unfortunately gives no reference.

> "I felt that it was better to live right than to live wrong; and
> as to caring for the interests of others instead of my own, the
> condition of the suffering people around me, people with
> whom I had been so long familiar, and whose agony seemed
> to reach its climax about this time, undoubtedly affected me
> very deeply."[3]

Sandall, writing much later, asserts:

> "The deprivations of his early life, the misery that in his
> boyhood he had seen around him, his memories of children
> crying for bread in the streets—all helped to set up in his
> mind the purposes that later came to such fruitful issue."[4]

At thirteen Booth was apprenticed to a Unitarian pawnbroker where his associations with the miseries of the poor
were cultivated. Under the influence of Feargus O'Connor,
the chartist, Booth for a time became interested in revolutionary politics.[5] St. John Ervine suggests that ". . . it might
have been, had the Methodists not caught his fancy, that he
would have given to parliament what he gave to the penitent-form."[6]

But God did catch hold of William Booth.

William's father experienced a death-bed conversion at
which William was present. From this time on, William

became somewhat more interested in religion. At the age of fourteen he left the Church of England for the Wesley Chapel. Through his associations at the chapel with a number of godly believers, William Booth came to a personal experience of conversion at the age of fifteen. While attending the revival meetings led by the Rev. James Caughey, William determined "'God should have all there was' of him."[7] His life was transformed into one of concern for the salvation of the lost. He was well acquainted with his pawnbroker clientele who must have seemed to Booth to be as lost as anyone could get. However, now he saw them in a new light, as Ervine informs us.

> "A halo waited for the frowsiest head that came on Monday morning to pledge the suit that had been redeemed on Saturday night! This shuffling drunkard, pawning his shirt, might become the prisoner of Christ, the serving soldier of the great Jehovah. That wretched woman, verminous and vile, could be turned into a holy lover of her Lord. The very words 'pledge' and 'redeem' took other and fine meanings for the young pawnbroker, who could, without strain on his imagination or abuse of speech, see in these mean bargains sacraments of the salvation which could be freely enjoyed by all who cared to receive it . . . ."[8]

Now Booth spent every moment he could in preaching and witnessing to the lost. His methods were unusual and often unappreciated. One time he brought a motly group of toughs to a chapel meeting and sat them in prominent pews. He was promptly reprimanded. At seventeen William became a local preacher taking engagements on Sundays. One of many local preachers engaged by the Methodist Church, his opportunities to preach were quite limited. He turned to street meetings and to have more time for this resigned as a local preacher. About this time, c. 1847 on, reform fires burned in Methodism. Booth's resignation was seen as rebellion against the Methodist Church and sympathy with the reformers. Booth's ticket of membership in the Methodist Church was not renewed and he was virtually expelled. Approached by the reformer Edward Harris Rabbits, he preached at the reform chapel in Binfield Road, Clapham, where he became the preacher on April 10, 1852.

Unlike William, Catherine's spiritual sensibilities were positively influenced from early childhood. She could read by age three and began her education in earnest by age five. Her major reading text was the Bible.[9] Her home life itself instilled in her strong moral standards based on spiritual principles.

> "It was to her mother more than to any other human influence that Catherine owed the early awakening of the strong moral sense inherent in her nature. She tells that from three years of age and onward there were sometimes tears at goodnight time, and the 'confession' of something the child thought 'wrong.' She could not go to sleep until her tender spirit felt forgiven and comforted with a sense of God's love. Her mother never excused the fault, nor attempted to explain away the child's distress. Conscience was a reality before babyhood was well passed."[10]

In 1833 the Mumfords moved to Boston in Lincolnshire where her father, John Mumford, zealousy threw himself into a newly formed temperance movement. Discussions by leaders of the movement were conducted in the Mumford's home and Catherine listened intently to these views and contributed her thinking, first as a child and later as one of the group.[11]

At age twelve Catherine attended a school for girls whose principal was a lady who attended the same chapel in Boston as the Mumfords. Catherine reveled in her studies. At fourteen she was taken with a severe case of curvature of the spine and school attendance ceased, but she continued her studies on her own. She read much on doctrine and Church history. She is reported to have read the translated works of Mosheim and Neander. Her daughter also reports that "Finney's writings and biography, his lectures on theology in particular, and other theological books were first read through and then perused and annotated."[12]

Catherine was on her back for almost a year, but the spinal problem began to correct itself. Just before Catherine turned sixteen, the Mumfords moved to London, making their home in Brixton. Catherine's daughter considers this a great event in her mother's life.

> "Hungry for knowledge, for reason's certainties, as she has been, she now longs for an inner witness: the *rest* of certainty in the soul's secret place. Her thoughts begin to turn inwardly to herself."[13]

> "Now, on the threshold of her seventeenth year, questions arise, disturbing, insistent, related to her own heart. Has she the assurance of her *own* salvation? Knowing so much *about* God and man's conception of Him, does she know Him by *personal revelation of Him* to her own soul? This for her now becomes the supreme question; her whole future hangs upon the answer."[14]

Catherine is quoted by her daughter:

> "I said, 'I will never rest till I am thoroughly and truly changed, and know it as any thief or great outward sinner....' I refused to be saved by logic . . . faith is not logic, but logic may help faith. . . . It seemed unreasonable to suppose that I could be saved and not know it."[15]

> "One morning, on waking, Catherine turned to her hymn-book and read:

> My God, I am Thine,
> What a comfort divine
> What a blessing to know that my Jesus is mine!

> She says, 'the words came to my inmost soul with a force and illumination they had never before possessed. It was as impossible for me to doubt, as it had been before for me to exercise faith. [Notice here that Catherine herself emphasises lack of faith as the crux of the matter for her.] I no longer hoped that I was saved; I was certain of it. The assurance of my salvation seemed to fill my soul."[16]

This happened on June 15, 1846, and now she could become a member of the Brixton Methodist Church with a clear conscience.

A dispute in the Wesleyan Church in the autumn of 1846 led to a rupture in the church family. Catherine and her mother sympathized with the reformers, and Catherine, who freely voiced her opinions, found that her ticket of membership was withheld from the Wesleyan Methodist Church. Catherine and her mother began to attend a reform chapel at Binfield. When not feeling well she attended a Congregational Church closer to home.

At this early period of her life, her position on women's equality in the ministry was clearly and preciously enunciated, a position which The Salvation Army would take from its very beginning. Respecting the preacher at the Congregational Church, a Dr. David Thomas, she found herself in disagreement with him when he preached a sermon Catherine believed to be derogatory to woman as a moral being. She wrote the following to him.

> "... in your discourse on Sunday morning... your remarks appeared to imply the doctrine of woman's intellectual and even moral inferiority to man. . . . Permit me, my dear sir, to ask whether you have ever made the subject of woman's equality as a *being*, the matter of calm investigation and thought? If not, I would, with all deference, suggest it as a subject well worth the exercise of your brain. . . . So far as Scriptural evidence is concerned, did I but possess the ability to do justice to the subject, I dare take my stand on *it* against the world in defending her perfect equality. And it is because I am persuaded that no honest, unprejudiced investigation of the sacred volume can give perpetuity to the mere assumptions and false notions which have gained currency in society on this subject, that I so earnestly commend it to your attention. I have such confidence in the nobility of your nature, that I feel certain neither prejudice nor custom can blind you to the truth, if you will once turn attention to the matter."[17]

Among the new acquaintances Catherine met in the reform movement was the same Mr. Rabbits who had befriended William Booth. Catherine and her mother were members at the chapel in Binfield Road when William Booth came to preach. Catherine was much moved by William's sermon. She met him at Mr. Rabbits' home and several other times, and friendship soon turned into affection of a deeper nature. So it was that these two very strong individualists, with not only personal but very emotional spiritual experiences of faith, were brought together. Their individualism and personal and emotional experiences of faith were to set the tone for Salvation Army expression and understanding in years to come.

Sandall gives a concise history of Booth's movements from this time. Concerned with the instability of the reform movement, Catherine Mumford suggested that he might become a Congregational minister. He was about to enter a training institution when he had problems with the doctrine of election. In November of 1852 he accepted a position as preacher at Spalding, Lincolnshire. However, still bothered by a lack of stability in the reform movement, he remained unsettled.

He found this stability in the Methodist New Connexion which he joined in 1854. He was appointed to the London circuit. In the New Connexion Conference of 1855 (Sheffield), Booth's evangelistic effectiveness was recognized as he was appointed to this work. On June 16, 1855, William and Catherine Booth were married. William conducted revivals for the next two years and very successfully. Some of the older ministers thought that this popularity might not be good for him and at the Conference of 1857 (Nottingham) he was withdrawn from evangelistic work and appointed to a circuit. He accepted the new appointment with reservations. He was ordained in the Conference of 1858 (Hull) but reappointed to a circuit. He went to Gateshead from 1858 to 1861. It was here at the Bethesda Chapel that so many decisions for Christ were made that it earned the name of "The Converting Shop."

At this time Catherine took a more personal interest in the ministry. She and William had come to know a Dr. and Mrs. Palmer who had traveled to England from the United States to conduct revival meetings during a time of recognized spiritual renewal in much of England. Mrs. Palmer was severely criticized for speaking from the pulpit and Catherine wrote a powerful pamphlet supporting the right of women to preach. It was here also that both William and Catherine determined that they must preach the doctrine of Full Salvation as popularized by John Wesley and strongly encouraged by the Palmers. In the Conference of 1861, Booth was again denied appointment to the field of evangelism. Convinced that his call to this field of ministry was a divine call, and unable to work out a compromise which would have allowed him to perform evangelistic duties, William Booth resigned. His resignation was accepted at the Conference of 1862 (Dudley).

From 1862 to 1865 William and Catherine Booth labored in the Revival Movement referred to by Edwin Orr as "The Second Evangelical Awakening." Orr argues that this was a revival begun in the United States which spread to England. The Palmers, who had become friends of the Booths at Gateshead, were leaders in this movement. Booth and his wife traveled widely and preached with great success in the churches in Cornwall and the provinces until the Methodist Conferences shut the doors of their churches to the Booths.[18] With few exceptions this revival movement was opposed by the Church of England and by the principal Methodist Churches.[19]

However, this spiritual awakening of 1859 brought into being the Home Mission Movement and, through it, the East London Special Services Committee which called Booth to East London. George Pearse of the East London Special Services Committee invited Booth to take part in religious services being conducted at the Garrick Theatre,

Leman Street, Whitechapel.

While Booth did not remain in the East of London at this time, the experience seemed to give him greater assurance that things were working out for a definite end. *The Revival*, the journal of the revival movement, contains a letter from W. Jones Hayden to John Stabb that reported successful meetings in a tent belonging to the East London Special Services Committee that had been pitched in a Quaker burial ground in Whitechapel, East London. Booth is mentioned as laboring in this endeavor. A further report indicated that William Booth had decided to give himself to this work in East London, the first public notice that Booth might remain in the East of London. In a short time, Booth took over the leadership of these missioners and organized a Christian Revival Association. In 1867 it became The East London Christian Mission, having changed its name from The East London Revival Society,[20] or The East London Christian Revival Union, depending on whether you are looking at the mission's first printed document or its ticket of membership and temperance pledge card. Both names appear respectively on these. By the end of 1869 branch missions had spread beyond the East End. In the September issue of the mission's magazine, *The East London Evangelist*, Booth announced a new name to describe this broader boundary: The Christian Mission. The first number of the 1870 magazine was titled, *The Christian Mission Magazine*.

The organization of the Mission was based on the conference model. By 1877 there was disenchantment with this form of government. Many believed it was too slow in arriving at decisions because it encouraged lack of agreement. According to Sandall, a meeting of the Conference Committee plus superintendents and evangelists was called for the 23rd and 24th of January 1877. Sandall reports:

> "The conclusions reached, without a dissenting voice, were that government by committees was too slow and round-

about; that decisions were continually required upon important matters; that theirs was a war, anyway; that the annual Conference should be continued, but as a council of war and not a legislative assembly."[21]

The conference was officially abandoned at its meeting from the twelfth to the fourteenth of June, 1877. The Conference Committee was given up. William Booth was given power to accept and appoint all evangelists. More consciously than ever before, the military nature of this new government was recognized and accepted. Sandall quotes from the conference minutes the words of William Booth:

> "We have been called [he said] by the arrangement of Divine Providence to be officers and leaders in His army, and we are met to consider how we can best advance the interests of that army."[22]

Sandall concisely summarizes this transition in government.

> "The process by which The Christian Mission adopted a military form of government and thus prepared itself for transformation into The Salvation Army was truly democratic. That its form of goverment should be military was decided by the special meeting of the Conference committee (January 1877); was ratified by the following Conference (June 1877) and legalized by the War Congress (August 1878), each body exercising the powers it possessed and its inherent freedom of choice."[23]

While the process of the transitional details occurred precisely, the evolution of the idea came to consciousness quite gradually. Sandall quotes Booth on the process that resulted in The Salvation Army.

> "We tried, for eleven years, various methods. We tried many plans. . . . Gradually the Movement took more of the military form, and finding, as we looked upon it, some four years ago, that God in His good providence had led us unwittingly, so to speak, to make an army, we called it an army, and seeing that it was an army organized for the deliverance of mankind from sin and the power of the devil, we called it an army of deliverance; an army of Salvation—The Salvation Army."[24]

According to Sandall the new name was legally recorded on June 24, 1880. In this endorsement the renaming is given as "'on or about the First day of January, One thousand eight hundred and seventy-nine.'"[25]

Booth reports that the Mission began the year 1878 with 30 stations and 36 evangelists and ended the year with 75 stations and 120 evangelists. By the end of 1879 there were 130 corps in operation and nearly 200 officers from Glasgow in the north to St. Helier's, Jersey, in the south.[26] Officers increased from 120 in 1878 to 3,602 in 1886.[27]

The number of officers grew quickly as the Army spread to other parts of the United Kingdom and then beyond. Commissioner Railton and his company of one woman officer and six women soldiers officially opened the Army work in the United States, along with a convert made on the voyage, on March 10, 1880.[28] Ireland was also invaded in 1880.[29] The work was established in Australia in February of 1881. The work in the United States and Australia was begun unofficially somewhat earlier as salvationist soldiers (laypeople) traveled to these countries and began to conduct worship services and other Army ministries. Having begun the work, they wrote to the General and asked that officers be sent to take charge. This happened in Canada. Its official opening in August 1882 had been preceded by Army meetings conducted earlier by soldiers who had migrated to Canada. The first Army meetings in France were conducted in March of 1881. Switzerland was invaded in December of 1882, and there the Army experienced some of the most cruel persecution in these formative years, a persecution approved of by the government and in some cases even organized by public officials. India and Ceylon were invaded in September of 1882. The Army flag was unfurled in Sweden in December of 1882. South Africa was invaded in February of 1883. The work was begun in St. Helena in May of 1884. In the beginning of 1883 the Army began work in

New Zealand.

The first International Congress, held May 29 to June 4, 1886 brought together Army forces from Australia, Canada, France, India and Ceylon, New Zealand, South Africa, Sweden, Switzerland and the United States. There were also Indians from Canada and the United States, Chinese from the United States, Germans and Italians from London, and Hollanders who wanted the Army to begin work in their country.[30] The General informed the Congress that there were 1552 corps (churches), 3,602 officers (ordained clergy), and that 28,200 meetings were held weekly, and nineteen different *War Crys* were being published.[31]

From 1886 to 1890 Salvation Army work began in the following countries: Argentina, Belgium, Denmark, Finland, Germany, Holland, Italy, Newfoundland, Norway, Uruguay, West Indies. From 1891 to 1895 the work began in British Guiana, Gibraltar, the Hawaiian Islands, Hong Kong, Iceland, Indonesia, Japan, Rhodesia, and Spain. From 1896 through the early 1900s operations commenced in Alaska, Barbados, Bermuda, China, Malaya, Malta, Mexico, the Philippines, Russia, St. Lucia, Trinidad, and the West Indies. In a little over ten years the Army had spread to some forty-two countries outside the United Kingdom.[32]

With the War Congress of 1878, the mission movement became an army formally. Terminology was borrowed from the British Army and Sandall asserts that the General ". . . stated that he had obtained more practical help from the regulations of the British army than he had from all the methods of the churches."[33] In the formation and conduct of this Army ". . . there was to be no difference between men and women as to rank, authority and duties. The highest positions were open to women as well as to men."[34]

According to the first book of regulations, the C.O. was the commanding officer or evangelist in charge of the corps (mission station or church). He was entitled to be called the captain, his assistants were to be lieutenants. They were also called F.O.'s or field officers. An S.O. was a staff officer who assisted the field officers in some particular aspect of the corps work.[35] Today, commanding officers may be lieutenants, captains, and majors. These ranks are given usually according to years of service. The ranks of "Lieutenant-Colonel" and up are given on the basis of additional responsibilities, usually in administration of a wider spectrum of Army services.

In The Salvation Army, church membership was referred to as soldiership and church members as soldiers. In the early years conditions of membership were implied in the rules regarding who could or could not sit on the platform. Sandall, quoting the rules, writes:

> "No-one was to be allowed to do so who 'did not take the most earnest and active part in the service from first to last; habitually neglected outdoor work without reason; whose dress three weeks after conversion was not in perfect harmony with orders; who used drink or tobacco a reasonable time after conversion; who was not accustomed to speak when asked six months after conversion; or who in any way discredited the Army, or who was not perfectly obedient to officers.'"[36]

Today there are two kinds of membership available to those interested in belonging to The Salvation Army. One may become an adherent, in which case the Army is simply acknowledged as the place of worship for the individual. By witnessing to a conversion experience and being willing to live as a Christian and to take on the additional standards of conduct as abstinence from intoxicating drinks and tobacco products, one may become a soldier, which permits the member to wear the Army uniform and makes the member eligible for local officership (lay leadership positions).

There was a semblance of uniform in the Army even from the early Mission days as evangelists dressed somewhat alike. This uniform became more military in appearance with the advent of the Army, but the uniforms were anything but uniform. Personal taste and imagination had great license in the mode of dress of the early Army. Uniforms were standardized gradually, and today commissioned officers wear regulation uniforms. However, some soldiers still improvise without strong criticism from their leaders.

As Salvation Army corps grew in numbers, further organization of the many corps was made necessary. Corps were organized geographically. In the *War Cry* of September 18, 1880, the General divided the Army into seven divisions with an officer in charge of each division and having the rank of major (although a captain might be a divisional officer).[37] As the Army continued to mobilize, additional ranks and divisions came into being. Now the Army is organized around the world into territories. In the United States there are four territories: Eastern, Western, Central, and Southern. Each Army territory has a territorial commander, usually with the rank of commissioner, but at times with the rank of colonel. Each territory is divided into divisions with a divisional commander in charge of each division. Usually the divisional commanders are majors or lieutenant colonels, although a captain might still be put in charge of a division. Each division is comprised of a number of corps. Some divisions have camps and social welfare departments that are set up to meet specific and widespread needs. To administer the division a divisional headquarters is set up and to supervise the divisions there is a territorial headquarters with various departments and bureaus. The divisional commanders are comparable to the district superintendents of the Methodist Church and the territorial commanders to bishops. There is one general who is the international leader of The Salvation Army. His office is at International Headquarters in London, England from which the world-wide work of the Army is administered.

Commissioned officers, who are the ordained clergy of The Salvation Army, are trained in Schools for Officers'

Training or Training Colleges. The course is two years in duration and subjects such as bible study, preaching, psychology, social work, business administration, etc., are offered. Training continues beyond the two years and many officers go on to earn college degrees.

In addition to the commissioned officers who are ordained clergy, there are various lay leadership positions referred to as non-commissioned ranks. The Corps Sergeant Major is the lay leader of the senior corps (adult activities) and the Young People's Sergeant Major is the lay leader of the youth corps (young people's activities). There are many sergeant ranks depending on the size and activities of the corps and there are rules and regulations attached to all of these ranks defining the responsibilities of these leaders.

As an Army, the officers in charge are truly in charge. They are augmented and assisted by advisory groups, but there is very little voting and electing done in the Army. While there are advisory boards comprised of soldiers and advisory boards comprised of community leaders, ultimate decision-making rests with the officer in charge. The Salvation Army is a religious order that operates on strict autocratic principles.

The Army's flag first came into official use at the Coventry Corps in England where it was presented by Mrs. Booth. Up to this point many banners were carried in processions with scriptural texts and injunctions written upon them, but now the Army had its own flag and Railton wrote:

> "'The use of flags has done more than anyone could have imagined to bind all our soldiers together and to encourage and develop the spirit of enterprise and resolution.'"[38]

The Army's ordination of women was a most significant departure from traditional church practice. Another significant departure was the decision not to observe the sacraments. In the early Mission years baptism and communion were practiced; however, the practice was increasingly questioned by the Booths. It was finally decided that the sacraments were neither necessary for salvation nor scripturally obligatory. The tendency to misunderstand the ceremonies concerned both William and Catherine Booth. Sandall quotes Mrs. Booth and the General respectively on this issue.

"Another mock salvation is presented in the shape of ceremonies and sacraments . . . men are taught that by going through them or partaking of them, they are to be saved. . . . What an inveterate tendency there is in the human heart to trust in outward forms, instead of seeking the inward grace! And when this is the case, what a hindrance rather than help have these forms proved to the growth, nay to the very existence, of that spiritual life which constitutes the real and only force of Christian experience."[39]

And the General is quoted as saying:

"Neither water, sacraments, church services nor Salvation Army methods will save you without a living, inward change of heart and a living active faith and communion with God and faith in what He says, and an active, positive, personal consecration of yourself and all you have got to help Him who hung upon the cross to fill the world with salvation and bring lost sinners to His feet."[40]

Though an Army in principle and practice, The Salvation Army considered itself nonetheless part of the Universal Church of Christ. Sandall quotes the General in an address of 1884:

"The Salvation Army is not inferior in spiritual character to any organization in existence. . . . We are, I consider, equal everyway and everywhere to any other Christian organization on the face of the earth (1) in spiritual authority, (2) in spiritual intelligence, (3) in spiritual functions. We hold "the keys" as truly as any church in existence."[41]

This assertion continues to be voiced throughout the ranks of The Salvation Army around the world, for today it is an international religious denomination. From what has been said above, Methodism is likely to have had a strong influence on this new denomination. How much of an influence is the question to which we now turn.

Chapter III
The Source of Salvation Army Theology

I t is clear that both William and Catherine Booth were heavily influenced by Methodism from the very beginning. Though independent in much of their thinking, the basic tenets of the Methodist faith were not something with which the Booths took issue. Methodism had made its mark on both of them and would make its mark on the Army they were to begin. Here the first position of this study is established, namely, that Army theology is a direct derivative of Methodist theological thought.

The theological formulations of doctrine espoused by The Salvation Army are not in any significant way different from the statements of faith of nineteenth century evangelicalism and specifically as it was expressed in Methodism. This conclusion is supported by comparing the Methodist Church and the Methodist New Connexion showing that these two groups were not separated by any disagreement in theology and that The Salvation Army was not in theological disagreement with the New Connexion. Considering Booth's formative relationship with both Methodism and the New Connexion, it will become clear that Salvation Army theology is a derivative of Methodist theology with no essential differences.

It was the question of church government that led to the separation of the Methodist New Connexion from Wesleyan Methodism. Salt, in his memorial on the New Connexion in 1823 asserted:

> "As Englishmen, our excellent constitution, and the general practice of dissenters, taught us to claim for our people, a participation in our church government, a voice in the enactment of its laws, (those laws by which we were individually to be ruled), and a share in the management of its temporal concerns."[1]

While Methodist laymen were content to give Mr. Wesley unconditional control of the Methodist movement, they believed that he would leave behind him a form of government ". . . which should embrace preachers and people in one common privilege and interest."[2] This hope was destroyed when Wesley framed his poll-deed. Salt said of it:

> "This poll-deed, or bill of rights, is exclusively the preachers' and excepting a few necessary regulations for the holding of conference, supplying the circuits, and providing for the demise of the connexion, there is no security, restriction, or in short any thing which can be called reciprocal in favor of the people."[3]

Negotiations failed and separation was unavoidable. The governmental system was so corrupt as far as the reformers were concerned, that to have any part in its perpetuation was to act against the eternal interests of the cause of God.[4] Both New Connexion writers and mainline Methodist writers agreed that the first split among Methodists had nothing to do with doctrinal issues.

> "In the plenary inspiration of the Holy Scriptures; in the Deity of Christ; the Personality and Godhead of the Holy Spirit; in the Fall of Man and the consequent depravity of our race; in the universal efficacy of the Atonement and the freeness of Divine mercy; in the necessity of repentance and a believing reliance upon Christ for salvation; in Justification by Faith to the utter exclusion of human merit; in the privilege of entire sanctification; in the necessity of holding fast faith and

continuing in good works; in the immortality of the soul, the resurrection of the dead, the general judgment, and the distribution of rewards and punishments; in the eternal happiness of the righteous and the endless misery of the wicked; and in every other evangelical doctrine we are identified with the parent community."[5]

". . . the grand cause of separation was that of church government; . . ."[6]

As we have already noted above, Booth's separation from the New Connexion was not due to any doctrinal differences. Booth felt called to evangelistic work. Expecting to be appointed to evangelistic work at the Conference of 1861, he was instead reassigned to a circuit. Unable to comply with the decision of the conference he resigned and in time founded The Salvation Army. Since the New Connexion had no essential disagreement in theology with Wesleyan Methodism, we may conclude that Booth had no theological problem with Wesleyan Methodism.

As expected, the influences of the New Connexion upon the Army are quite clear. With respect to politics the New Connexion took the following position.

"As a religious community, we neither have interfered, nor do we profess to interfere, with political concerns; like the kingdom of our Lord and Master, the Methodist New Connexion has no relation to the political affairs of this world."[7]

From the Army's inception, it has been against regulations for any officer, even the General, to take any political stand officially. No statements can be made on behalf of politicians or political parties.

Certain organizational features of The Salvation Army seem to be results of New Connexion influence. The Methodist New Connexion organized the Beneficent Society for ". . . the relief and support of disabled, aged, or superannuated preachers in the Methodist New Connexion, and the widows and orphans of preachers."[8] This could very well have been the inspiration for The Salvation Army Retired Officers' Fund. It is highly probable when one looks at the title of the formal document outlining the Beneficent Society: "Rules, Orders and Regulations, for the Government of the Beneficent Society."[9] The Salvation Army has *Orders and Regulations for Officers, Orders and Regulations for Corps Officers,* and orders and regulations for almost every activity and leadership position, lay and commissioned.

The doctrinal statement of The Salvation Army has its roots in the doctrinal statement of the East London Christian Revival Society which William Booth joined and eventually led. This society became the East London Christian Mission, then The Christian Mission, and finally The Salvation Army. The doctrines of the East London Christian Revival Society were seven in number. They were retained almost word for word by The Christian Mission, except for the second doctrine of the Society which was divided into two doctrines by the Mission. The Mission went on to adopt three more doctrines, making eleven in all, which were retained when the Mission became The Salvation Army. While these three have no corresponding doctrinal statements in the Society doctrines, they do correspond, and quite closely, to doctrines of the Methodist New Connexion. The following will record the Methodist New Connexion doctrine first, marked N.C., The Salvation Army doctrine corresponding to it next, marked S.A., and last, the Revival Society doctrine corresponding to the other two and marked R.S.

1. (N.C.) We believe in the existence and perfections of the Supreme Being.

2. (S.A.) We believe that there is only one God who is infinitely perfect; the Creator, Preserver, and Governor of all things; and who is the only proper object of religious worship.

3. (R.S.) We believe that there is one only living and true God; the Father, the Son, and the Holy Ghost—three persons in one God—equal in power and glory; and the only proper object of religious worship.

---

2. (N.C.) We believe that the scriptures of the Old and New Testaments are given by Divine inspiration, and form a complete rule of faith and practice.

1. (S.A.) We believe that the Scriptures of the Old and New Testaments were given by inspiration of God and that they only constitute the Divine rule of Christian faith and practice.

1. (R.S.) We believe that the Scriptures of the Old and New Testaments were given by inspiration of God, and are the only rule of Christian faith and practice.

---

3. (N.C.) We believe in the Divinity of Christ, and in the Personality and Godhead of the Holy Spirit.

3. (S.A.) We believe that there are three persons in the Godhead—the Father, the Son, and the Holy Ghost—undivided in essence and co-equal in power and glory.

3. (R.S.) We believe that there is one only living and true God—the Father, the Son, and the Holy Ghost—three persons in one God—equal in power and glory, and the only proper object of religious worship.

---

4. (S.A.) We believe that in the person of Jesus Christ, the Divine and human natures are united, so that He is truly and properly God and truly and properly man.

3. (R.S.) We believe that in the person of Jesus Christ the Divine and human natures are united, so that He is truly and properly God, and truly and properly man.

---

4. (N.C.) We believe that Adam, by his fall, involved all his posterity in guilt and depravity, and that Christ has made an atonement for the sins of all mankind; and that there is no other name given under heaven by which we can be saved.

5. (S.A.) We believe that our first parents were created in a state of innocency but by their disobedience they lost their purity and happiness and that in consequence of their fall all men have become sinners totally depraved and as such are justly exposed to the wrath of God.

4. (R.S.) We believe that all mankind, in consequence of the disobedience of Adam, are sinners, destitute of holiness, and justly exposed to the penalty of the divine law.

---

4. (N.C.) (See immediately above.)

6. (S.A.) We believe that the Lord Jesus Christ has by His suffering and death made an atonement for the whole world so that whosoever will may be saved.

5. (R.S.) We believe that the Lord Jesus Christ has, by His suffering and death made an atonement for the whole world, so that whosoever will may be saved.

---

5. (N.C.) We believe that repentance is absolutely necessary to salvation.

7. (S.A.) We believe that repentance toward God faith in our Lord Jesus Christ, and regeneration by the Holy Spirit are necessary to salvation.

6. (R.S.) We believe that repentance towards God, faith in our Lord Jesus Christ, and regeneration by the Holy Spirit are necessary to salvation.

---

6. (N.C.) We believe that justification is by grace through faith, and that he that believeth hath the witness in himself: that it is our privilege to be fully sanctified in the name of the Lord Jesus Christ, and by the Spirit of our God.

8. (S.A.) We believe that we are justified by grace through faith in our Lord Jesus Christ and that he that believeth hath the witness in himself.

10. (S.A.) We believe that it is the privilege of all believers to be "wholly sanctified" and that their "whole spirit and soul and body" may "be preserved blameless unto the coming of our Lord Jesus Christ" (I Thessalonians 5:23).

---

7. (N.C.) We believe that all our salvation is of God, and that man's damnation is all of himself. Nevertheless, we believe that in the gospel plan of redemption, men are treated as rational accountable creatures: that 'it is God that worketh in us to will and to do of his own good pleasure'; and that we are to 'work out our own salvation with fear and trembling.'

---

8. (N.C.) We believe that it is possible for man to fall finally from grace.

9. (S.A.) We believe that continuance in a state of salvation depends upon continued obedient faith in Christ.

---

9. (N.C.) We believe the soul to be immortal, and that after death it immediately enters upon a state of happiness or misery.

10. (N.C.) We believe in the general judgment at the last day, in the eternal happiness of the righteous and in the endless punishment of the wicked.

11. (S.A.) We believe in the immortality of the soul in the resurrection of the body in the general judgment at the end of the world in the eternal happiness of the righteous and in the endless punishment of the wicked.

7. (R.S.) We believe in the immortality of the soul—in the resurrection of the body—in the general judgment at the end of the world—in the eternal happiness of the righteous—and in the endless punishment of the wicked.[10]

A casual reading of the doctrines of the Methodist New Connexion, The Salvation Army of 1878 (and the Christian Mission prior to this date), and the seven doctrines of the East London Christian Revival Society dating back to 1866 show that they contain essentially the same statements of faith. The New Connexion statement of faith contains one doctrine, no. 7, concerning free will in the statement of sin and damnation as well as redemption and salvation, which does not appear in either The Salvation Army or the Revival Society statements. The Revival Society statement contains no doctrine on justification by grace through faith or on sanctification as these were added later in the evolution of the Society to The Salvation Army. It is interesting to note that these later doctrinal statements of The Salvation Army (i.e. nos. 8 and 10) bear a close connection to their New Connexion counterpart, no. 6. Salvation Army doctrine 9, although similar in content to New Connexion 8, is quite different in wording.

It is clear from the above that Salvation Army doctrinal statements in the formative years of its growth were in no essential way different from the New Connexion statements. That the doctrines of the Army and mainline Methodism are compatible is further supported by an author somewhat critical of The Salvation Army. In speaking about the Army's statements of faith he writes:

"Here again let me point out these are the cardinal doctrines of the Methodist creed. Original sin, universal redemption provided by Christ, the necessity of the Spirit's grace, justification by faith, the witness of the Holy Ghost, entire sanctification, and a judgment to come were the great subjects about which our fathers so mightily preached."[11]

It is quite clear that Salvation Army doctrine is a derivative of Methodist doctrine.

Chapter IV

Seed Ground
for an Army

B y the mid-nineteenth century, England was seething
with turmoil while breaking ground for the modern
world of the twentieth century. It was the social and
cultural soil of Victorian England that nurtured the seeds
which grew to be The Salvation Army. We need to understand this English soil which encouraged the ideas of this
peculiar Army if we are to understand the significance of
Army theology. The eighteenth century holds some helpful
insights for this study.

The Enlightenment brought into being a period of great
optimism which rested upon a very high view of man. The
pre-industrialist, Adam Smith, an eighteenth-century
Scottish moralist and political economist, promoted this
high view of man. He asserted that man was fundamentally
motivated by self-interest, a self-interest which could be
educated to consider others. If so, the self-interest of each
person would produce the self-interest of all. Further, if self-
interest is the key to the interest of all, then free competition
and an open market are the proper economic atmosphere
and institution to bring into being the best for each individual and each nation.

Another eighteenth-century thinker, the philosopher Jeremy Bentham, concerned himself with the individual. His philosophy of Utilitarianism defined Adam Smith's self-interest. It was an interest in seeking happiness and avoiding pain. Ethically, regarding pain, "right actions are those which tend to diminish it, and . . . we ought to do what is right and not do what is wrong . . . ."[1] It is apparent that Bentham also held a high view of human nature. Like Smith, he asserted that the common good or the harmonizing of interest would ultimately be attained in a freely competitive market. This economic position was given official status by the chief economic thinker of the nineteenth century, David Ricardo. He believed that the concept of a free market was governed by a natural economic law which would assure the harmonization of interest on behalf of the public good.[39] Eighteenth-century social and economic philosophy exalted the individual. They gave man a prominence which was to have significant meaning in nineteenth-century England.

In addition to these economic and philosophic foundation blocks upon which Victorian society was to rest, the thinking of the seventeenth-and eighteenth-century scientist, Sir Isaac Newton, provided a scientific foundation for nineteenth-century England. Natural law was at the heart of Newtonian science and the Newtonian world view was one of the significant carryovers from the eighteenth to the nineteenth century. Newton represented the universe as essentially a machine which operated on set principles that could be understood and utilized to further understand life. Here was the empirical world of cause and effect moved by natural law, which natural law was the proper object of scientific inquiry.

As we found a relationship between Bentham's Utilitarianism and economic theory, so we find a relationship between Bentham and Newtonian science. Bentham's Utilitarianism was immersed in this mechanical view of the universe. He was able to simplify the complexities of human nature into one basic principle of action, utility, a principle emanating from the individual and determining a way of life for all individuals. In the nineteenth century, the focus of attention, was upon the world around man, but it was the individual who had become the prime actor. Explicitly, it was the outside world that was in the spotlight, but implicitly the individual dominated the whole stage of reality. Victorian England seemed to fulfill Genesis 1. Man now appeared to dominate creation.

Looking at Victorian England in light of the Industrial Revolution, it is not hard to understand why it embraced so fervently these eighteenth-century concepts which exalted man, encouraged an open and freely competitive market, and applauded free enterprise among individuals and between nations. With the Industrial Revolution, England became the first and only industrialized nation of its time. The English had opened a whole new dimension of civilization. England reaped the benefits of an industrial monopoly. Its economic, philosophic, and scientific concepts suited its advantages in the world. But, these concepts, combined with the Industrial Revolution, brought a radical change in nineteenth-century society.

With philosophical and scientific concepts of mechanization coming together in the Industrial Revolution, a new world view developed in England. Industrialization resulted in a totally new relationship between man and society. The order of the old feudal system which was somewhat preserved in the eighteenth-century concepts of nobility and gentility was gone. Unlike eighteenth-century society which was vertically ordered and where everyone had a place and knew that place with its responsibilities and obligations, industrialized society was made up of classes connected horizontally, each competing with the others for prominence, power, and wealth.

The landed gentry, still desiring the past with its order, continued to be the most affluent class. As investors they provided the capital for industrial development. However, this class was no longer lauded; it was rather criticized for receiving riches for which it had not labored. Benthamite Utilitarianism sounded the deathknell of the prominence of this class. It was now the useful who were to be lauded, and the nineteenth century did not look upon the landed proprietors as the most useful class. Individual performance was more worthy than the gain of inheritance, and with this emphasis on the individual, equality before the law was demanded. Work was a most worthy expression because it was useful. The administrator, the manager, the "captain" of industry moved England, and he belonged to the middle class.

The middle class gained power in government and took control of education as it guided Victorian England into the fastest, most extensive period of growth ever experienced by any nation to that time. It asserted that competition was one of the natural laws governing industrial development and profit. Competition was thought to bring out the best, the truest of everything. Profit in production was the ultimate badge of success and England was astonishingly successful, both as a nation and in the wealth of many of her individuals.

But this is only the positive side of the story. There was a price to be paid for this progress. Since the chief concern was profit, lowest production costs and highest possible sale prices were demanded. The human fodder that powered this economic-industrial machine of wealth and status was the navvy, the common laborer, the man of the working class who worked the hardest and longest for the least gain. He provided the cheap labor for production. Whole families, including children five, six, and seven years of age, labored long hours in the factories. Many families endured such poverty that they could not support their children and had to sell them into apprenticeship or servitude. Families that stayed together often lived in one room flats or cellars which lacked sanitary conveniences. Even worse, there were millions who had no jobs. They were uprooted from the land which was no longer the primary means of support, and transplanted to the city where either job or charity offered some means of receiving food and clothing, but where neither offered enough of the staples of life.

It is not that the Industrial Revolution brought poverty to England. There had always been poverty. Life was never easy for the peasant prior to the nineteenth century. But it was one thing to be poor while living on the land and quite another thing to be poor in the city. It was one thing to be poor while most others were poor, and poverty was accepted as somewhat a station in life with some mobility. It was quite another thing to be poor among people who were very wealthy and where wealth and success were supposed to come to the hard-working and enterprising, no matter what one's original station in life. In Victorian England, poverty was not only brought to social consciousness but increasingly questioned as to its causes.

Victorian England was a country of contradictions of which its people and its leaders were aware and by which they were greatly troubled. Beside incomprehensible wealth was incomprehensible poverty. Neighborhoods of mansions were juxtaposed with ghettos in which people daily died from starvation and the innumerable diseases associated with abject poverty. Opposite the entrepreneurs of the Industrial Revolution were the masses out of work or working for less than subsistence wages. Englishmen began to ask, why, in the midst of unprecedented economic growth leading to vast individual and national wealth, were there so many desperately poor people.[3]

Unfortunately, the Victorian social view did not provide a very satisfying answer. Kathleen Heasman describes this view in her treatment of Evangelicals and their social involvement in Victorian England. The ways to social and economic responsibility and success were self-help, character, and thrift.

> The poor were only helped if they were destitute; in most cases they had to enter the workhouse for relief, and the conditions there were such that they should compare unfavorably with those outside.
>
> This deterrent approach can be explained by the Victorian attitude that it was the duty of everyone to help themselves, and only in the last resort to appeal for outside assistance.[4]
>
> "... a man should, by his own efforts, provide for himself and his family, and ... he could do so by the careful and thrifty use of all his endowments. This was the attitude which had produced the self-made industrialist of the early decades of the century and it was the view that dominated the outlook of the middle classes and the higher paid workers throughout the century."[5]

To tell a working person who, along with his family, is starving, that success comes from hard work and individual effort is less than convincing, especially when one keeps working and growing hungrier. To tell the unemployed who cannot find work that hard work and individual effort will bring success is depressingly laughable, and the poor did laugh, in a very depressing way.

In addition to their physical poverty, there developed among them a moral, ethical, and spiritual poverty. Every form of illicit behavior was manifested in the impoverished masses, so much so that some of England's writers referred to Christian England as Heathen England. Whether they were looked upon in amazement, disgust, or compassion, there was great reservation in referring to them as Englishmen. They were regarded as misfits, people who should not *belong* to this sophisticated and proper social order. With the social needs of poverty, disease, ignorance, immorality—all rampant in the poorer classes—there was this cultural need resulting from disfranchisement. These people had no access to the benefits of their society and little hope for a brighter tomorrow. They had no home in their own land. It is not hard for one to understand the hopelessness that prevailed amongst the poor. They had no answers to their poverty, no resources with which to fight that which threatened their very existence. As a result they had little hope for the future. The hope of faith had no object and faithlessness found no shelter. For the poor, disfranchisement and hopelessness reigned as the feeling, emotive nature of man, was subjugated by the cold reason of a cause-and-effect world view.

The churches, especially, were concerned with the spiritual and moral depravity of the people. They expressed grave anxiety over the indifference of the masses toward Church. This was a sin of all ages, but in nineteenth-century England its manifestations took on the most appalling features reducing men, women, and children to human refuse, the gutter filth of society. Drunkenness, immorality, filth, and disease among the masses was epidemic in proportions, and separation from the Church was a conscious, intentional position held by the vast portion of the poorer classes. The Christianity of Christian England was aroused and drawn to the poor, and it was this spiritual soil in particular which brought forth the new religious movement known as The Salvation Army.

While the churches were the most involved group reaching out to the impoverished masses of nineteenth-century England, they were not necessarily the most effective workers among the poor. The rift that developed between the churches and the masses was never healed, not even by The Salvation Army. However, the Army was the only new religious denomination to come out of Victorian England, and it was comprised largely of the poorer classes. It achieved significant success in reaching out to the masses.

The Army grew up not only in conjunction with the social and cultural influences of Victorian England but also in direct relationship with the efforts of the English religious community. We must look at the religious soil which nurtured and helped shape this new Army.

From the 1790s through the early 1800s, Britain was among a number of countries which experienced the "Awakenings" of Evangelical Protestantism. "Throughout the mid-Victorian age the evangelical movement was the strongest religious force in British life."[6] By 1800 it came to dominate the culture of the middle and upper classes.[7] Evangelicalism established a religious consensus that

> ". . . limited the intellectual alternatives open to the potential convert by filling his mind with the question of his own Salvation, with the absolute need for personal religious experience and with the hell that lay in the background."[8]

More specifically, the essentials of Evangelical Orthodoxy included

> ". . . the fall of man, the divinity of Christ, man's redemption through Christ's atoning death, the inspiration as a whole and in every detail of the Bible, and the everlasting torment of sinners."[9]

Except for some minority positions, the existence of God, a divine Christ, an inspired Bible that told of God's self-revelation, and future life ". . . were as entrenched among the axioms of ordinary Englishmen in 1837 as fifty years before."[10]

However, while there was a religious consensus clearly evident in the early part of the nineteenth century, it was not so much a consensus based on true piety or spirituality as it was based on social respectability.

> "Respectability, in eighteenth-century usage referred to social position, and denoted a person of established standing, enjoying certain amount of prosperity. Its increasing use during the nineteenth century as a term denoting moral worth,

regardless of position, was thus one aspect of the democratisation of English society: it was a part of the bourgeois concept of a free, competitive and mobile society, with a hierarchy based on achievement rather than birth."[11]

Ideally, a person was now free to pursue prosperity and he was assured that if he worked hard enough success would come and with it respectability.

For those who claimed English respectability, church-going was the thing to do. It went together as an indication of their social standing. It served the purpose of displaying the religiosity of the English people. Sunday morning from 11:00 a.m. to 12:45 p.m. became the sacred expression of national respectability. Church-going was politically and socially motivated, and not necessarily an indicator of intrinsic religious spirituality.[12] Further, respectability, while claimed to be a possibility for all, was defined in such a way that it became an impossible achievement for the great masses of English people. Manual work did not qualify for social respectability even if it were done with such morally upright characteristics as industry, self-discipline, self-education, and wholeheartedness. Respectability became a middle-class tool to justify its own class dominance and working-class subservience.[13] McLeod put the religious consensus of Victorian England and its idea of respectability in pungent relief when he observed that

"It was a measure of Evangelical achievement that for much of the century so many members of the upper and middles classes felt bound to attend church regularly, to observe Sunday, and to censor their conversation. It was a sign of the limits of this achievement that so much of this was hypocrisy."[14]

The message of the church took on such middle-class and evangelical emphases as individualism, personal religious experience and diligent work.

"It promised improvement for all through a combination of education and increased moral effort, and it frequently challenged existing conceptions of religion—usually on behalf of Evangelical Protestantism, though sometimes from a utilitarian or rationalist point of view."[15]

The churches were not a source of much encouragement to the poor.

A consideration of the various social classes in Victorian London and the churches they were apt to frequent will further describe the social and rational basis of religious expression. In the upper class, Anglican membership and high levels of church attendance predominated. McLeod summarizes the social atmosphere of West End society. They possessed

> "... a sense of minute distinctions of social status and of their reflection in local geography; a sense of family and of family traditions; an awareness of the appropriate and the "proper" and a willingness to impose social sanctions on those violating these standards."[16]

If the upper class had the highest percentage of church attendance in London over-all, McLeod asserts, regarding the upper middle class, that,

> "In terms of church-going this was the most "religious" class, and it was probably here that the effect of nineteenth century "seriousness" was most profound, though in the upper class "religion" was less escapable, and in the lower middle class there were more people in isolation from unbelievers."[17]

Superficially, nineteenth-century seriousness expressed itself in terms of an abundance of religious practices like family prayers, regular church attendance, and a distinct Sunday behavior. These were regarded as giving evidence of proper reverence or at least a sense of propriety in general. At its deeper level, seriousness was "... a belief in Truth, and the necessity of discovering what it was, and in Duty, and the necessity of following it."[18]

Between the superficial and the deeply serious, there existed a wide variety of beliefs. They ranged from an utter repudiation of orthodoxy or convention to a strong suspicion of anything that even hinted of unorthodoxy. By the eighties and nineties variant views of theology were quite entwined with middle-class values as many old taboos were dropped and many churchgoers

"... adopted a more extroverted and life-giving Christianity, in which 'character'—good citizenship, hard work, and a balanced personality—was the thing most highly valued. This was one of the chief themes in upper middle-class religion of this period; the others were the sense of service, ..., and the desire for beauty, reverence and mystery in worship which was one of the sources of the growing strength of Anglo-Catholicism."[19]

Like the upper class, the upper middle class had no place for the evangelical characteristics of the faith. A humanism, which left little place for God's direct involvement in human events, political and social concern, education and philosophy and concern for and habits of hard work, dominated religious thought. The questions raised by men like Maurice on the incompatibility of God's love and the doctrine of hell took root among believers and unbelievers. Almost everyone saw evolution "... as a slow and painless process, whose course had been arranged by a kindly deity, christian or not, who aimed at the perfection of the race."[20]

The solid middle class represents the middle-class stereotype:

"... conformism; a belief in work; an intolerance of failures, loafers, eccentricity, frivolity; a respect for the 'practical man', defined as the astute and unsentimental man of business; 'deferment of gratification,' together with a devotion to the interests of his own family as the supreme end."[21]

This segment of the middle class usually retained the evangelical character of religious expression. It was made up of those people who had comfortable incomes but neither the education nor the culture to qualify for West End Society. They were "... identified by Matthew Arnold as Moody's and Sankey's audiences and 'the main body of lovers of our popular religion.'"[22] Speculative philosophical and scientific theories and the doubts and questionings of higher critics and churchmen who questioned the old, accepted, doctrinal understanding of the church were not appealing to this class of society.

Living in the suburbs but part of the working class were the Black-Coated Proletariat. They were petty capitalists,

> ". . . clerks, shop assistants, commercial travelers and elementary school teachers concentrated around the northern and southern limits of the County of London, and in the newer suburbs outside."[23]

This person ". . . saw 'culture,' 'education,' and interest in general as being among the marks of his own section of society, separating him from his fellow proletarians."[24] In his religious views as well as social and political views, he was most drawn by the emphasis on individual moral effort as might be expected of people who are in a position to move up on the social scale. Church preference would place them predominantly in the nonconformist denominations.

The working class consisted of the impoverished masses. They were neighborhood centered, aware of only their own small, insecure world. Characteristics of this extreme parochialism ". . . included indifference to questions of abstract principle, a low valuation of education, and non-participation in organisations."[25] People in a life and death struggle needed to stick together to get over the crises that faced them daily.

> ". . . those who felt powerless in a world dominated by mysterious alien forces tended to respond by withdrawing into a more local world, within which their words and actions were of some consequence, and questions concerning the general nature of society, let alone of the universe, they tended to dismiss as irrelevant speculation; the arbitrary ruler of their world was not God but Fate."[26]

Church attraction was not a force in the lives of these people. Only Roman Catholicism held a large number of work-

ing-class churchgoers, and this was due to the migration of
Catholics to England from other lands. On the whole the
people of the working class were ignorant of religious doctrine and extremely anti-clerical. Church-going was repudiated and churchgoers thought to be self-righteous and superior in attitude. It was not easy for the impoverished person
to go to church, and McLeod argues that the few working-
class people who did attend were usually from a segment of
the class that was better maintained and who could look
ahead to the possibility of something brighter. Concerning
their spiritual values,

> "Most of those working men, . . . , who made a sufficiently
> radical break from the life of their workmates to make them
> wish to join a church adopted highly evangelical beliefs, in
> which the blood of Jesus was more prominent than the ser-
> mon on the Mount, and in which great symbolic significance
> was attached to abstinence from drink, oaths and sometimes
> tobacco."[27]

The above represents a late nineteenth-century church
community with a wide variance in theological beliefs.
However, it was a church which was governed, as was society, by middle-class values. It was concerned about the heathenism of the masses, but, like its secular counterparts, it
stood above the poor, reaching down to the have-nots to
share wisdom and give counsel. Its respectability and seriousness were self-serving and were considered cold, callous,
lifeless, and boring by the needy. The great social problem of
Victorian England, disfranchisement of the poor, was also
the great spiritual problem of the Victorian Church.

George Scott Railton, Booth's first lieutenant in Mission
days and the first commissioner of The Salvation Army, in
writing Booth's biography, asserted:

> "The English National Church, eighty years ago had
> reached a depth of cold formality and uselessness which can
> hardly be imagined now. Nowhere was this more manifest
> than in the 'parish' church."[28]

Railton considered things somewhat better in the Methodist Church but not significantly so.

> "Here the services were, to some extent, independent of books; earnest preaching of the truth was often heard from the pulpits, and some degree of real concern for the spiritual advancement of the people was manifested by the preachers."[29]

Bramwell Booth, then second general of the Army, wrote of the religious attitude in the days of the Army's beginning: "The evangelistic pulse at this time had run down."[30] He asserted that the Army

> "... was not the product of its age, except in the sense that it was a sharp reaction from the ideals of respectability and complacency which to an unusual degree governed English life at that period."[31]

Those in the Army were not the only critics of this problem in the religious community.

Reverend Prebendary Wilson Carlile, founder of The Church Army, wrote:

> "In the early eighties the sound apostolic idea of using keen working men and working women to win their fellows was, unfortunately, thought to be somewhat revolutionary inside the Church of England. In my view, the problem of indifference was even greater then than it is now; and yet, inside the Church, any enthusiasm or really aggressive effort was speedily crushed by excessive respectability."[32]

The bishop of Melborne is quoted in an Army periodical of 1884-5.

> "Very readily do I admit that it would not be difficult to find a Christian Church which is not obnoxious to criticism; and even more readily that our own comparative coldness, formality, and want of elasticity are shamed by the enthusiasm and practical resource of The Salvation Army."[33]

Mrs. Booth, in the same periodical, asserted of the Church in general:

"Whatever has caused it, it is a fact that the masses of the people have come to associate ideas of stiffness, formality, and uninteresting routine with our church and chapel worship; and if we are to be co-workers with God for them we must move out of our jog-trot paces, and become all things to them, in order to win them. If they will not come inside our consecrated buildings, we must get at them in unconsecrated ones, or out under the canopy of heaven."[34]

The Salvation Army, along with other church groups, labor movements, university movements, and government movements, did go to the poor. All kinds of schemes were proposed to bring a better life to them, but, with the advent of The Salvation Army, a new way of religious life entered upon the scene of Victorian society, a society which was ready for it. While Bramwell Booth would argue that The Salvation Army was not a product of its age, his recognition that the Army was a sharp reaction to the values of Victorian Society is in itself admission that it was in one sense a product of its age. Nineteenth-century culture made a place for the idea of such a thing as The Salvation Army and the idea, once uncovered, became a reality.

Many of the cultural characteristics of Victorian England were positive influences on this idea of an Army of God. In England something new was happening; it was a time of essential change. There were great problems with no simple solutions. This encouraged questions, new ideas, debates. With the reconstitution of the social make-up in Victorian England, not only the problems but the proposed solutions involved the whole of the social spectrum. In all of this change, turmoil, and anxiety, a group of religionists, mostly from the lower classes, dressed in uniforms, marching through the streets, beating drums, and blowing horns, while not much appreciated was, however, not unthinkable. In fact, as government officials began denying the Army access to the streets because of the commotion caused by their opponents and critics, it was the English newspaper,

The Times, one of the great voices of English society, that protested these decisions arguing the right of the Army as English people to freedom of the streets and calling for their protection from the unlawful mobs who created the havoc. After all, was this not the great day of the individual—individual effort, individual creativity, industry? Every individual had rights, especially the right to equal treatment before the law. This peculiar movement called The Salvation Army should at least have a voice, since it was made up of free people.

Worldwide conquest, in whatever sense, was the heart of the colonial spirit, and colonization had been part of the heritage of England for a number of centuries. With the Industrial Revolution this world consciousness and conquest was ever more encouraged and compelling. Here was an ideal setting for a new Army. When Booth says that he gained more from the regulation books of the British Army than from the methods of the Churches, he is implying more than rules and regulations.

Even the materialistic nature of the industrial world view of nineteenth-century England was not without its benefits to this new Army. Though this view had little place for the supernatural, as man and reason dominated thinking, it also had few answers for the problems it generated. The belief that man could do anything if he put his mind to it was brought under increasing criticism as millions were shackled in the bondage of misery and poverty and ever more encouraged in their heathenism. By the time the Army came to town, some people were ready for a more apocalyptic mentality. Perhaps God was a way out, and perhaps he did care and was still personally involved in the human predicament.

The Army took the evangelical faith and clothed it in ideas which opened up its most precious treasures not only to the common people, men, women, boys, and girls, but even more to the most depraved. A people without vision and hope, aliens in their own world, began to think that there might be a light shining at the end of a long, dark tunnel. Perhaps there was a home for them.

Part II

A Theology of Grand Ideas

Chapter V

Introduction

Though Salvation Army theology was a derivative of Methodist thought, it was clothed in grand ideas. What was it that made this theology that was not at all original, grand?

First and foremost, the theology of the Army was grand in its formative years because it worked. The preaching and teaching of the Army reached down to the very will of a people and brought out inspiration, commitment, hope, purpose, and love. People responded by the thousands to form this new movement. Additional thousands became financial and advisorial supporters of the Army, and this happened around the world in a very short time. The possibility of true success which this theology preached was in great measure illustrated through the movement, for the movement did succeed.

If this writing were only about a brief past, these ideas might be referred to as grandiose; ideas that promised much, flowered for a short time, and then wilted in the demanding atmosphere of reality. However, this theology still calls forth the same kind of commitment in The Salvation Army of today, no matter where it is found around the world. The significant work which this theology preached and taught became a reality in the movement, and it continues to be a reality in the present. Time and success have made the theology a theology of grand ideas no matter what happens in the future.

The theology of the Army dealt with the ultimate issues of eternal life and death, heaven and hell. It dealt with the ultimate solution to every human problem: God's plan of salvation accomplished by his son, Jesus Christ, and carried out by his people, the Christian Church. Had the Army believed that they would indeed win all of the people of the world to Christ and usher in Christ's earthly reign, we might well call their ideas grandiose. There is no doubt that the Army believed that God could save the world. It was convinced of a powerful God, an Almighty God. Yet, the Army did not consider as primary whether or not the world would be saved. It considered as primary the fact that Christians were needed to work to save the world no matter what the outcome.

In a most unique way the Army opened up these promises to a universal audience, the "whosoever." It took the promises of new and abundant life through Christ and clothed them in the human garb of the lowly and unlearned and made the common man responsible for the salvation of the world. The soldiers believed themselves called to exert every possible effort to provide God with the means by which this universal salvation might be offered to the world. In this urgent partnership with God, an intimate sense of the presence of God was brought back into public life. He was seen as not only caring about poor sinners but actively and personally involved. He had called forth an Army and was calling forth soldiers.

The world was opening up. It was there to win for Christ. Anathema to the great part of the ruling middle class — certainly to the aristocrats — and to most of the poor themselves, this theology took hold and weathered the storms of protest and criticism to break out into the sunshine of approval and appreciation. There was admiration and praise both from the people who joined the movement and those who watched it work. It is the substance of that theology and what it meant to the disfranchised that we will now investigate.

Chapter VI
The Doctrine of Salvation

S alvation was central to Salvation Army theology. However, the peculiarity of the Army's view of salvation did not come from doctrinal formulation. There was no new theology here.

In the first article of the only issue of *The Salvationist*, the new title for *The Christian Mission Magazine*, Booth strongly declared:

> We believe in the old-fashioned salvation. We have not developed and improved into Universalism, Unitarianism, or Nothingarianism, or any other form of infidelity, and we don't expect to. Ours is just the same salvation taught in the Bible, proclaimed by Prophets and Apostles, preached by Luther and Wesley, and Whitfield, . . .[1]

Continuing, Booth wrote, "We believe the world needs it, this and this alone will set it right. We want no other nostrum - nothing new."[2]

Booth could lump Luther, Wesley, and Whitfield together and do it comfortably because neither he nor his earlier mission nor his later Army was concerned with fine points of doctrine. The early Army was concerned with basic truths. Booth, writing in an 1868 issue of his mission magazine, *The East London Evangelist*, made clear that the concern of his magazine would not be with different opinions and minor points of doctrine and discipline. He would avoid these concerns ". . . so that Christ and Him crucified be held as the only ground of a sinner's hope here and hereafter."[3]

This idea of salvation created a tension with the thought of the day. As stated earlier, the Victorian mind argued for self-help. Individual effort, genius, and industry were the tools of success. Ignorance was the enemy of success and so education and cultural refinement were considered to be the answers to the social dilemma of heathenism and debauchery in the lower classes. In the early years of the nineteenth century, charity was not widely practiced and individuals were encouraged to help themselves. By the 1890s, Kathleen Heasman pointed out, "It was beginning to be realized that social distress was not necessarily the fault of the character of the individual but quite often was caused by economic factors entirely outside of his control."[4] Even with the growing awareness that character was not the only structure of life that needed reshaping, the social conscience of the nation was moved to experiment with many different social schemes in an effort to find the right formula for success. The Salvation Army argued that salvation was the answer. Sinners needed saving. True they needed help; they needed training, encouragement, and support. But this would be to no avail unless they were made conscious of their alienation from God and their need of a savior who could forgive them of their sins, recreate their spirits, and live in and through them.

The Army found a tension between itself and the prevailing thought of the day, not only in the recognition of sin and the understanding of salvation, but in the understanding of sin as well. As mentioned, self-interest was lauded in nineteenth-century England. The Army argued that sin was universal, that each and every person was born a sinner, totally depraved, and that the essence of that sin was self-interest. In

The Christian Mission Magazine of 1877, Mrs. Booth clarified the nature of the universal sin inherent in human nature.

> This is just the point where human nature has failed from the beginning. Our first parents fell here. Their consciences were on the right side, but their wills yielded to the persuasions of the enemy. THIS IS SIN. The committal of the will to unlawful self-gratification.[5]

Selfishness as the essence of sin was given official theological recognition in the Army's doctrine book of 1881: ". . . all are *at heart* alike, given up to the gratification of their own selfishness, and utterly indifferent to the claims of God and the happiness of mankind."[6] The Army was certainly receptive to the idea that selfishness was not only a universal sin problem, but the cause of all social problems. In *The Darkest England Gazette*, the official newspaper of the Army's social operations, a writer asserted: ". . . my own personal experience has convinced me that the real cause of all the present miseries and difficulties is the selfishness of man."[7] He went on to argue:

> In the East End as well as the West End, amongst all classes, *wherever* there is no restraining or hallowing religious influence, I find a mean, contemptible, damning, selfish spirit, which undoubtedly is the very bottom and real cause of all of our misery.[8]

The leading voices of English social concern cried for natural effort in retraining and sharing the wealth of learning. They scolded a belligerent class for its lack of self-discipline and inordinate appetite for the things of the flesh. The Army called for a supernatural work of salvation that could only be accomplished by God working through his people. The poor were not the only ones who erred. The whole of English society was missing the mark, including secularists who had little use for religion and the Church. Salvation alone was the ultimate answer to the problem of sin, and the Army believed that this was God's plan, established from the beginning of all beginnings. It also believed that God had called the Army to cry out the message of salvation in a wilderness of evangelical apathy and moral degradation. The Army stood against some of the general trends of its day, and yet succeeded.

The Army's theology was fueled by its consideration of the life to come. Its concern was for the essence of being—the soul—whose existence transcended time. Its ministries were set by its conviction of ultimate life and ultimate death, heaven, and hell. Even more, the parameters of those ministries included the whole world and the whole man. It is no small wonder that an Army with this ultimate concern could keep in focus and indeed regard as its priority the souls of individual people as well as the most basic aspects of their personal lives. The Army chose to care about the world through a concern for each of its inhabitants and sought to lead all into an experience of salvation. Here is a theology of noble purpose, but very difficult to take seriously even today. Yet, this theology made believers out of thousands around the world. The Salvation Army became an Army of Salvation.

While the Army engaged in a wide variety of ministries directed at many social ills, it was a movement directed to the one primary goal of soul winning, the goal to which everything else was secondary. Bramwell Booth argued that the Church ought to work in those areas only directly related to the Church's task which was explicitly:

> . . . blessing the poor, relieving the distressed, and saving the bodies and souls of the people. Its supreme work is to save men, whether they be Socialists, Radicals, Liberals, or Conservatives, from their sins. The quality of goodness is the great determining factor in the moral advance of the people.[9]

Soul-winning was William Booth's call to the ministry. It remained his passion during his own formative years of turmoil and frustration. Once entering the East End of London, he would forever more pursue soul-saving results. They were the consuming passion of his Christian Mission: "To live, to move, to grow; to be a power amongst men, a light in the world, the flaming sword of God—that is our calling."[10]

> We want the burning love to dying men which feels with a terrible heart-pang every sinner's misery, and forgets danger and difficulty and discouragement in the deathless agony to pluck brands from the burning. We want to be bigger, grander, holier, more god-like men and women, and we must be if we are to do what God expects of us.[11]

In the very beginning of these mission days, Booth and his colleagues considered this passion for soul-winning a universal call to all Christians. In discussing the nurturing of converts in *The Christian Mission Magazine* the author asserted:

> Make them question the ground of their religious hopes. Make them understand that true godliness is practical benevolence, and that they must at once become followers of Jesus, and go in for a life of self-sacrifice in order to do good and save souls, or else give up all hope and title to being Christians.[12]

The mission felt the pressure of fields ready to be harvested and the need for more laborers.

> We are more and more struck as time passes us with the extreme difficulty of the task we have in hand. Thousands upon thousands listen to the Mission every day in the open air. Multitudes of these are impressed even to tears, and yet it is positively terrible to reflect how few after all of those who have been accustomed to neglect the house of God are really gained to our certain knowledge for Christ every year. While in no wise disposed to discouragement, we feel very deeply the need of increased prayer, power, effort, and labourers, that larger, very much larger, results may be realised.[13]

This urgency for soul-winning as the primary task of the Church continued to be the primary emphasis as the Mission became The Salvation Army. General Booth wrote:

> "Salvationism means simply the overcoming and banishing from the earth of wickedness, inward and outward, from the heart and life of man, and the establishment of the princi-

ples of purity and goodness instead."[14]

This Salvation War on behalf of humanity is not waged in any piecemeal fashion. Our aim is not to help poor, suffering, sinning man a little in this corner and then in another, but to lift him entirely out of the gulf in which he is plunged, and to emancipate and bless him, in every phase of his being, for time and eternity.[15]

Everything must be brought into the service of this soul-winning. "Read, give, pray, talk, sing—do anything you can. Everything that seems likely to make people know the truth about themselves and Heaven, and Hell."[16] The editor of *The Officer*, 1893, wrote:

We have no hobbies . . . unless it be a hobby to want to save the largest number of souls with the highest possible salvation in the quickest space of time by the best imaginable methods. That is . . . the sum and substance of our mission.[17]

For the Army it was the lostness of man that prompted the divine call to the ministry. Colonel Lawley wrote:

In the face of these missions of beckoning hands, calling voices, sad souls, burdened hearts, darkened minds, rebel throngs, is not our duty clear? Cannot you and I hear the voice of the Son of God asking us to pray to the Lord of the harvest? Nay, more than that, cannot we hear Him asking us to ask others to leave all and follow Him?[18]

As the Mission considered this call to soul-winning to be incumbent upon all Christians, so did The Salvation Army. The doctrine book of 1881 warned of the failure to win souls.

. . . if we do not, we shall certainly be charged with the responsibility of their destruction[.] Oh, let us pray and preach, and visit and persuade men, lest at the last great day their blood should be found in our skirts.[19]

An ex-Salvation Army officer wrote of his first impressions of this movement: "It appeared to me that here was a people wholly and entirely devoted to the salvation of souls and the extension of the kingdom of Jesus Christ."[20]

The Army was aware that this sense of duty and mission was considered to be radical by many other church people and believed that it was the reason for much of their criticism.

> They think that if they ATTEND a place of worship, READ their Bibles, and SAY their prayers, that this is all that is meant by FOLLOWING Him; and such people being condemned in their own hearts as they see others persecuted for doing what they neglect, often become the most vehement denouncers of all zeal and enthusiasms in the service of God. They call it fanatical and extreme to speak of sacred subjects at what they judge unsuitable times, and even go so far as to denounce as blasphemy that which is pleasing to God.[21]

However, the Army was convinced that God wanted the world. The opening sentences of the first publication of *All The World* read, "Why should not Jesus Christ have 'all the world'? Has anyone got any sufficient reason? Do any of our readers know of any?"[22] The Army answered the question with a resounding NO!

> "Chimerical,""enthusiastic,""extravagant,""Utopian," do you say these calculations and exhortations are? They may be to you; no doubt they are to many, but we Salvation Soldiers believe them. They are not more so than a certain book called the Bible, or was the solemn farewell commandment given by the great Captain of our Salvation — the Lord Jesus Christ.[23]

The Army affirmed a worldwide, soul-saving crusade.

> Our end, our aim, is to gain the world for God. Of all things, I despise a selfish religion which considers my family, my children, my circle, and doesn't lift a little finger to help stop the millions outside rushing down to Hell. Whatever religion this may be, it is not Jesus Christ's. His heart went out to every sinner.[24]

As Army operations broadened to become a worldwide mission, the need for laborers became acutely more pressing. "Yes; *men are wanted*. We recognise the need within the sphere of our own influence. We feel it almost every hour of our lives; at times it overwhelms all others."[25] From where were these soul winners going to come? Colonel Lucy Booth said they were to come from sinners, sinners saved by grace. "We need them beyond and above all the prayers we have each prayed with which to obtain them, but we must pray harder, call out louder, wrestle longer, *for we must have them!*"[26]

Any and all seekers after souls were welcomed in the Army. Mrs. Booth gave the invitation eloquently.

> If the soul is worth all the sacrifice which Jesus made of His glory, of His rule, and dominion in Heaven, the laying aside of the glorious estate in which He sat at the right hand of His Father from all eternity, surely we can sink our little dignities and pomposities for it!
>
> . . . here is a war in which you will win celestial honours — honours that will last forever. Will you enlist? We take all recruits in this Army. If you have a HEART TO LOVE, come along. We want men and women indifferent to all other aims and ends but the extension of the Kingdom of Jesus. . . .[27]

While some churches looked for more ministers to ordain and some movements looked for sophisticated volunteers to redeem the poor from their poverty and heathenism, the Army went to the people to save them through Christ that they might become soul-winners themselves. Railton reported on this Army practice. "The humble labourer, without any great speaking ability, and often involved in a struggle to earn the barest livelihood for himself and family, was taught how to share in seeking the Salvation of men."[28] Some outside the Army came to agree with the wisdom of such an approach.

> The Salvation Army teaches the churches a lesson here. The Salvationists reach the people through the people; they make all their converts workers. Here surely is one way to win the people. Give them an interest. Make them responsible for something. A Church with working men sharing its responsibilities and taking part in its official as well as in its spiritual life would of a certainty lay hold of the people.[29]

For the Army the day of harvest had come. Colonel Lawley asserted that given enough evangelists, every country would be invaded by Salvation Army forces. "The crowds all around us, in addition to the millions of other countries, are like the corn, ripening fat, and unless gathered quickly will rot and die on the plains."[30]

As the theology of the Army was able to retain both a heavenly and earthly concern, so was it able to do a similar thing with the very nature of the doctrine of salvation. The theology of the Army was able to keep together a very emotional and mystical notion of salvation with a very sober and rational notion of salvation. In more traditional terms, Army theology sought to keep together faith and works where each of these concepts was considered in somewhat radical terms.

The Army accepted a kind of direct, mystical communication from God to man in this experience of salvation. The Holy Spirit

> "... does not confine Himself to sending messages to men through His *people*, or through books, but He, Himself, goes straight to people's hearts and so influences them as to make them feel what He wants them to do."[31]

For The Salvation Army, the doctrine of salvation was essentially spirit, a deep inner conviction of the heart. However, it found expression in a rational call to urgent labor. It was the change in the hearts of people that prompted plans to bring about change in more hearts.

The object of salvation was the heart, the spirit, the nature of a person, so that this heart might be fixed upon Christ. This was an emphasis carried over from the earliest of mission days as this quote from The East London Christian Mission Magazine indicates.

> In this actual closing with Christ consists the only or chief ground of hope we have for sinners; without it, all mere resolutions and head knowledge will avail but little; therefore, we attach but little importance to instructing men's minds or arousing their feelings, *unless* they can be led to that belief in

Christ which results in the new creation.[32]

The central place for this personal encounter with Christ was the penitent-form, often referred to as the altar, the place of prayer, the mercy seat, or the mourner's bench. Bramwell said of it:

> The penitent-form was ever the central spot in life to our beloved Founder. From the time he was sixteen years of age, everything in his affairs led up to it—every interest was made to bend to it. To bring souls to that place of decision where rebellion against God is renounced, and His will is embraced, was his supreme object.[33]

Why the penitent-form? Railton wrote:

> The General was always extremely opposed to the use of any plan other than that of the Penitent-form, lest there should be any distinction made between one class and another, or an easier path contrived for those who wished to avoid a bold avowal of Christ.[34]

The penitent-form, where "a bold avowal of Christ" was to take place, points out the active, urgent, and instantaneous character of conversion. In order to sensitize sinners to their sin and need of salvation, "Death, judgment, hell, eternity, God's justice, the terrors of the law should steadily be kept in view."[35] The brighter side of salvation such as mercy, pardon and peace were for a later date.[36] At the penitent-form,

> "Instant decision, salvation or sanctification *on the spot*, are the sum and substance of the moment's work. Immediate results must be aimed at, struggled for and claimed."[37]

As emotion-packed as this salvation experience was, it contained a very rational and sobering element. It required a *real* change of character from worldliness to godliness. Sin was real, there was no denying that. However, to the Army, salvation was also real and powerful.

> ... it is the "old-fashioned Gospel" that tells man he is thoroughly bad and under the power of the devil, that drags out

the very hidden things of iniquity to the light of the great judgment throne; that denounces sin without mercy, and warns men of eternal wrath to come, unless they repent and believe in the only Saviour; the Gospel whose goodness does not consist in the suppression of all but sweet sounds of love, but in the plain, straightforward, ceaseless announcement of the great truth; the Gospel of a crucified Saviour, who shed real blood to save men from real guilt and a real danger of a real hell, and who lives again to give a real pardon to the really penitent, a real deliverance from the guilt and power and pollution and the fact of sin to all who really give up to Him a whole heart and trust him with a perfect trust.[38]

The Army believed that Satan was deceiving a good part of the Church about this truth.

He has succeeded, first, in deceiving them as to the standard of their own religious life. He has got the Church, nearly as a whole, to receive what I call an "Oh, wretched man that I am!" religion. He has got them to lower the standard which Jesus Christ Himself established in his Book—a standard, not only to be aimed at, but to be attained unto—a standard of victory over sin, the world, the flesh, and the devil, *real, living, reigning, triumphing Christianity!*[39]

Man played a most active role in the perfecting of his salvation. However, as rational and sobering as this aspect of salvation was, emphasizing human will and perseverance, salvation remained essentially a *work of God*. In addition to requiring a convert to exhibit a godly life, the Army required the convert to feel in his heart that his sins were forgiven and he was indeed a Christian. This was no staid salvation accomplished by a ritual of good works, nor was it an emotional leap in the dark trusting in blind faith that God would catch the convert. Conviction and repentance had to be accompanied by the assurance of salvation, and this assurance was a *work of God*. To the seeker, the Army implored:

Search *til you find* the pearl of great price, backslider. Do not give up because you fail at the first attempt. That is not how the men of the world gain their fortunes or their honours. No; they seek til they find. You have been to the penitent-form before, but you did not find what you sought. Search *til you find*. That sort of spirit cannot be denied. Sometimes God *delays* our blessings, so that when received we may value them the *more*.[40]

The Army warned the Christian worker:

> *Never tell them they are saved, if they don't think so.* When a man gets saved, God will tell him about it; and then he will not need you to tell him so. But encourage him to go on seeking; urge him to go and deal with God alone, and come again. *Get his address;* have him *visited. Go after him yourself.*[41]

To discuss salvation as a personal and individual experience which goes beyond rational assent to a mystical kind of certainty conveyed by God to man, and to regard this as absolutely indispensable for a valid spiritual experience, is to argue that "Being" is foundational to "Doing." K. S. Inglis, discussing the Army and its doctrines has observed that "For an officer, . . . , it was not enough merely to assent to these doctrines. They must possess him."[42] In the materialistic age of Victorian England, where reality seemed to be quantifiable and all mysteries within the reach of human reason, where the value of things was assessed by a utilitarian standard (i.e., their usefulness), the Army argued the supernatural back into the natural without deprecating either. Very much a child of its day, it preached a *real* assurance of salvation. This assurance was subjective in its certainty but it was objective in the command that the life of salvation be lived for all to see. If you are, you will do. Colonel Lucy Booth put it this way:

> What "more of God" can enable us to be! We are something, all praise to Him!–we are cleansed through the precious Blood of the Lamb—we have been chosen to be His disciples— we are already called by His name! We are so much we used not to be—ever so much we never thought we ever could be.[43]

Then, with more of God, what we can then DO![44] This sense of Being, being God's person individually and being God's people as his Army, sustained the Army even when the results of its doing were minimal. Inglis picked this up in his study, which includes a section on The Salvation Army.

> Good Salvationists never forgot that their task was to win souls for Christ; and even if they won few, the sense of being a community set apart for this purpose contributed to the fellowship of an Army Corps.[45]

Above all, love was to characterize this being. The love of God was preached as the very essence of the Being of a Salvationist as it should be for every Christian. The spirit of love was to inspire and clothe all of the efforts of the Army. In the General's words: "Fight with the spirit of love. Not of anger, of hatred, of condemnation; but of LOVE. Pure, beautiful, patient, enduring, happy love."[46] Because salvation was presented as a real experience, carrying with it the assurance of a divine work done in the heart of a believer, the love sought after was a knowledgeable love rather than a sentimental concern. It was a love with substance and direction, a special, peculiar love which also could only be given by God.

> . . . this bringing of love, such as I am speaking of, into our lives, we cannot make it, we cannot manufacture it ourselves, and cannot manifest it til we have received it. It is something that comes from God.[47]

While being was foundational to doing, the doing of the Army was not depreciated in any sense. The work of the Army played a paramount role in the way the Army lived out its understanding of salvation, even as the call to a real character-changing experience had a practical effect upon the emotion packed concept of a spiritual conversion accomplished by God and testified to by his Spirit.

The doing of the Army was intensely practical. Booth's great social scheme, published in 1890, was titled *In Darkest England and the Way Out*. For a short time, it caught the fancy and financial support of many English people. Its scheme was to establish city, farm, and overseas colonies. City colonies would provide shelter and labor for the masses of unemployed in the cities, and goods would be produced for sale to the city's poor at more affordable prices. The over-population of the cities would find an answer in the farm and overseas colonies where people, forced off the land by the economy, could return to the land and produce goods and raw material for use throughout England. It has been suggested by some that at this time Booth came as close as he ever would to viewing economic and environmental factors as the causes of England's misery, rather than the universal depravity of human nature.

Booth's social scheme never fully developed, though much of the Army's Harbor Light mission work and its Adult Rehabilitation Centers working with the homeless, the alcoholic, and drug addict are direct results of the city-colony concept. It seems that this was a grandiose idea, and yet the spirit of practicality and common sense that undergirded it spawned hundreds of successful social programs and causes. It was this intensely practical character that kept the feet of the Army's concept of salvation firmly planted upon the ground of reality. This combination of an emotionally mystical spiritual experience with an intensely practical program of social assistance and caring made the Army's concept of salvation a powerful idea.

This social scheme and the establishment of the Social Wing of The Salvation Army as a distinct emphasis in the panorama of Army ministries illustrate the Army's appreciation for the effects of environment upon the individual. The Army was ever willing to reach out to the masses with a helping hand, whether or not they subscribed to its theology. However, the hope was always that this help might encourage the recipients to give the Army's message a listening ear. There is little doubt that the Army believed that its colonies would assist England, even if the people did not all accept the gospel of salvation. Yet, there is no evidence that this awareness ever dulled the Army's conviction that salvation through Christ was the only lasting answer to the miseries of a people, and anything short of salvation would only lead to eventual ruin.

For The Salvation Army, the sin of the world was considered to be a personal problem. Even when the Army's social scheme reached its greatest popularity, and when the Army branched out into more and more programs of social involvement and assistance, there was never any concept of social sin. At the turn of the century Sir Robert Stout, an eminent Englishman, said of the work of The Salvation Army:

> It seems to me, leaving out for the present any reference to its theology, that The Salvation Army has been based on this fact, that, if you are to accomplish any great work in dealing with humanity, you must make that work individual. Mankind cannot be saved in a mass; you must go to each individual man and to each woman; and if you wish to reform them, or to redeem them, you must deal with them individually; and I believe that that individual dealing has in a great measure made The Salvation Army successful.[48]

The Army was in full agreement with this observation. Its emphasis upon the individual went back to its earliest mission days. In its magazine, *The East London Evangelist*, it was written:

> The visitor who desires to take the "light of the world" to the dark homes of the poor, should remember that it is absolutely necessary that every unregenerate sinner should feel his condition before God to be a state of sin; otherwise it is impossible to believe in the necessity of a Saviour.[49]

Booth attributed his success to this preaching of a real, personal, and individual salvation. In an interview he responded to a question about his success.

> . . . If I were compelled to condense the answer to your question into a solitary sentence, I should say; In the insistence upon an actual experience of salvation, including a heart realisation and development of love to God and love to man.[50]

He went on to say,

> ". . . I have always regarded all theoretical opinions, and church ceremonials, and passing feelings as being subordinate, nay, as being *nowhere*, in comparison with a *personal realisation of Divine things.*"[51]

This idea of salvation requiring divine assurance and practical life-expression permeated with love and centered within the life of the individual, became a very compelling force. Here was a spirit which sought to compel people to consider the sin of the world as well as the sin of their own lives. This was one of the lessons Booth believed the Army had given to the world. It asserted that God's people

> . . . whatever they are called, must be the *Rebukers* of the world—the *Intruders* upon its selfishness and pleasure life— the *Demanders* from it of its dues and duty to God, its Maker and Judge. No greater mistake could be made than to suppose that our sole business with the world is to serve it or reveal to it the sympathies and benevolences of God. We are to condemn its sin and command its repentance and foretell its doom.[52]

A noted churchman of England quotes another respected colleague with reference to the Army and the work of the Church.

> "'The Salvation Army,' said Bishop Lightfoot, the wisest and most learned of our Prelates, 'has at least recalled us to the lost ideal of the work of the Church, the universal compulsion of the souls of men.'"[53]

It is not clear here whether Lightfoot means that the Church is compelled to seek to save the lost or that the Church is to compel the lost to at least listen to the gospel. However, both aspects were consciously pursued in the warfare of the Army. The Army's warfare was compulsory.

> "Wherever a true faith in the Gospel exists, The General's organisation of compulsory plans for the Salvation of souls will not only be approved, but regarded as one of the great glories of this life."[54]

The Army's program was to "compel" the attention of the lost.

> . . . all who really hear God's voice cannot but become alarmed as to the manifest danger that His warnings may remain entirely unheeded. When once any soul is truly enlightened, it cannot but put forth every devisable effort to compel the attention of others.[55]

The reader will understand better why this love is referred to as a love with substance. It was sober, serious, challenging, inspiring, and visionary. The Army was to "... *overcome, conquer, subdue,* not merely teach, but *persuade, compel* all nations, that is, all men to become the disciples of the Son of God."[56]

It was this spirit of compulsion that drove the Army into the streets to personally contact the lost and suffering.

> The Salvation Army is not content to stand upon the pedestals of dignity and far-off compassion, describing and commiserating the sins and misfortunes of the people, in the hope that they may in some undefined way come to a better state of things. It descends to them, goes down into the street where they are, and on to the level of actual human touch with them, and, appealing to them by means which they can appreciate, calls to the careless, startles the vicious and degraded, and lays hands on those who are spiritually sick and dying, and brings them to the Healer of Men.[57]

The Army did compel people to consider the gospel and to become soldiers whose lives were completely engaged in this salvation warfare. Not all were the dregs of society. There were those from the upper classes who joined the Army, often to the sorrow and despair of loved ones. This is illustrated in the words of a father who mourned the loss of his young daughter to The Salvation Army.

> . . . with respect to my child and to other young persons of whom I have heard, I fear the Army influence has a direct tendency to wean the converts from home associations and interests, under the idea that its work is paramount in importance to all other pursuits and obligations, and even to the known wishes of parents.[58]

Mr. Charlesworth went on to refer to a letter received from his daughter.

> . . . through it all there was the mournful evidence that she was the captive of the Salvation Army; that a father's love, a daughter's duty, a sweet home in which there was every indulgence and comfort, were not to be set in the scale against work in the Salvation Army.[59]

This call to global soul-winning was so explicit as to separate those with a genuine burden for this work from those inclined to a more traditional expression of religion. The Army was openly critical of the established Church and ever sought to maintain its distance from it.

> We refuse to settle down into places of worship such as might be agreeable to our people and their families, but insist upon the open-air stand and the place of amusement, where there may be little comfort, but where the most good may be done. We refuse to allow our officers to stay very long in any one place, lest they or the people should sink into the relationship of pastor and flock, and look to their mutual enjoyment and advantage rather than to the salvation of others.[60]

> We are not and will not be made a sect. We are an army of soldiers of Christ, organised as perfectly as we have been able to accomplish, seeking no church status, avoiding as we would the plague every denominational rut, in order perpetually to reach more and more of those who lie outside every church boundry.[61]

In this salvation war, God and man had come together dynamically and taken the offensive against the powers and principalities of spiritual darkness. A newspaper writer reported:

> The salvationists act as though they believe that the never— dying souls of men and women will be lost unless they are persuaded to accept Salvation through Christ, and they 'go out into the highways' to bring them into the Ark o[t] safety.'[62]

Bold and daring methods are required in any offensive campaign. The open-air street-meetings with instrumental bands and personal testimonies and the *drum* were among the most effective weapons in the Army's arsenal. While the drum offended many, it pushed forth the claims of this warfare in a most powerful way. Asked why the Army must use this terrible sounding instrument, the response was:

> Oh! the drum! We could not give that up. It is the drum that empties the Public Houses. The people at the bar are attracted by the noise, and come out to see what is the matter. Then some of them follow the march, and are taken hold of. The drum brings a good many to the Penitent Form.[63]

In this salvation war, offensive in character and global in dimension, there was a real cost of discipleship. A Major Wells from California reported:

> My heart is cheered. We are making the devil mad. Victory will come! Look out for some martyrdom here in the near future—it is to come, sure. Well, we are saved to die, and don't care much where our bones are buried.[64]

From India this report was given of the war.

> Sleeping on the ground under trees I don't mind, and you are so hungry by the time you get your food, that your hands go into the rice and curry of sticky dough without being asked twice. Thank God it isn't a sin to eat with unwashed hands.
>
> You can't take changes of clothing with you, as you sometimes have to swim across stretches of water, and are constantly wading. The filthy, stinky water you have to go through is the great danger, excepting the water you drink.[65]

For some, the cost of discipleship was too much.

> Owing to our adherence to this rigid military system, we are losing almost every year officers, as well as people, who, having lost their first love, begin to hanker after the "rights," "privileges,""comforts,""teaching," or "respectability of the churches." No one remains with us, or is likely to remain, whose sole object in life is not the attainment of the one purpose ever kept before the Army—the rescue from sin and hell of those who are farthest from God and righteousness.[66]

In this salvation war the primary word was always "attack." Booth, answering criticism of the Army's work in

Switzerland said:

> It is the same story everywhere; we are in the front of a life and death struggle against unbelief, drunkenness, and other vices which National Assemblies fear to grapple with, but which must be overcome if the nations are not to be handed over to ruinous debauchery and ruffianism.[67]

Christians must be doing something. Railton, writing Booth's biography, asserted: "The inexorable law to which he insisted that everything should bend was that nothing can excuse inactivity and want of enterprise where souls are perishing."[68]

> He proved that it was possible to raise up "Christian Soldiers," who would not only sing, or hear singing, in beautiful melody about "marching, onward to War"; but who would really do it, even when it led to real battle.[69]

Offensive warfare is warfare that presses the issue. It is a first-strike effort. Commenting on Acts 26:16 and God's command to his disciples to go into all the world, Mrs. Booth said:

> Not build temples or churches, and wait for the people to come to you, but "go ye"—run after them, seek them out—and "preach My gospel to every creature." Thrust yourselves and your message on the attention of men.[70]

"I sent thee as my herald, to shake them, arouse them, open their eyes, make them think, and realise the verities of eternal things."[71] "We are not to shrink from pressing the truth on men's attention for fear of giving offence."[72] *The Officer* records as one of the General's first principles this:

> " . . . while others were considering the best methods to be employed in order to reach the masses, we have been to the fore with the living fulfillment of the only practical answer to the question, viz., 'GO TO THEM.'"[73]

In the words of Mrs. Booth:

> We must fight with ignorance by enlightening it. We must come down to that measure of humiliation and sacrifice which is necessary to this. We must adapt ourselves. We must

> grapple with the condition of the people, where *they are*, put the arms of a loving sympathy around them, and weep tears of Christ-like compassion over them, pray for and reason with them, man to man, woman to woman, in hand-to-hand, face-to-face conflict.[74]

The unsaved masses needed to be shown Christ, alive and concerned. Without any smattering of blasphemy, these warriors intended, as far as possible, to be Christ to the suffering lost.

> We must contend with hatred and opposition BY LOVE, show sinners how God loves by our love, by our willingness to sacrifice and suffer for them; make them see it in our tears, in our prayers, in our trudging about after them....[75]

The biblical revelation that God loved the world of sinners enough to give his son for its salvation has been a source of hope and inspiration since the days of Jesus. However, the idea of God calling into being an Army of all kinds of people, most of low estate, even the lowest, to reach out to a whole world of sinners with the hope of salvation is more something about which fiction writers might write stories. When this happens in human history and is recorded as actual event we have a theology grand in concept and practice.

Chapter VII

The Doctrine of Sanctification

Except for the preaching of salvation from sin, there was no theological concern that received greater emphasis by The Salvation Army than the doctrine of holiness or entire sanctification. Even as the doctrine of salvation dealt with the ultimate issues facing a person, so this doctrine dealt with the ultimate issues within a person. How extensive is this experience of salvation? To what degree is there victory over sin? How is Christian perfection defined and how necessary is it? The doctrine of salvation focused on real change in heart and action. The doctrine of sanctification focused on deep change in the heart, so that Christian action might have divine, compelling power.

In the experience of salvation, the Army believed that a person was forgiven of all sins and became a true member of the family of God. In this salvation, the convert was free from sin, had the indwelling of the Holy Spirit and was bound for heaven. This was a simple understanding of sin. All people were sinners, but through conviction and repentance, motivated by faith in Christ, a sinner could gain forgiveness and establish a new relationship with God.

In the doctrine of sanctification, the Army recognized the much more complex nature of sin. There was more to this experience of being "saved" from sin. Salvation went only so far as to justify the sinner and regenerate his nature so that his concerns were turned toward God rather than being bound by sin. However, sin still had a place in the believer's heart.

The 1881 doctrine book argued that regeneration was imperfect.

> . . . there is still left hanging about the soul, and dwelling in it, many of the old, evil tendencies which, although brought under subjection by divine grace, still often rise, overcome, and drag him into sin.[1]

Wood asserted that,

> When the believer begins to pray for holiness, . . . the soul begins to see more and more of its own *vileness, deformity,* and inward *corruption.* God makes to the soul a more clear and painful discovery of remaining *impurity.*[2]

> . . . when a believer begins to pray for purity, he appears to himself to *grow worse and worse* . . . at this point there is much danger of getting discouraged, and giving up; here many fail at the very threshold of success. "*Blessed* are the *poor* in *spirit,* for theirs is the kingdom of heaven."[3]

The Christian Mission Magazine had given a clear description of those tendencies which still remained in the heart of the justified.

> . . . the enemies within, namely, self-will, self-preference, anger, peevishness, a puffing up at times, half-heartedness, desires after other things besides God, enmity against God's ways in saving souls, self-opinion, a wisdom arising from longstanding or consistent walking in the church for a long time, and a self-commendation on that account, an unlikeness to the genuine Christian, a love of preeminence, envy, uncharitableness, a judging spirit—these must be destroyed.[4]

This understanding remained part of Salvation Army theology.

While regeneration was imperfect, it was regarded as the beginning of sanctification. According to J. A. Wood, whose book on holiness was recommended to officers by *The Officer,*[5]

Justification and regeneration are concomitants and inseparable. Regeneration is the beginning or the lowest degree of
sanctification, hence, every justified soul is either *partially* or
entirely sanctified.[6]

Wood continued: "Justification and sanctification are perfectly distinct, although the beginning of sanctification is
inseparable from the justified state."[7] What was it that made
the one distinct from the other? Wood argued that it was the
nature of man and his sin, and he argued the point on the
basis of the whole tenor of scripture. His source was none
other than John Wesley.

> . . . Indeed this grand point, that there are two contrary
> principles in [unsanctified] believers—*nature* and *grace*, the
> *flesh* and the *spirit*—runs through all the Epistles of St. Paul,
> yea, through all the Holy Scriptures; almost all the directions
> and exhortations therein are founded on this supposition,
> pointing at wrong *tempers* or *practises* in those who are
> notwithstanding acknowledged by the inspired writers to be
> believers. [*Sermon on Sin in Believers.*][8]

Along with Wood the Army believed that the experience of
entire sanctification would destroy the nature that encouraged those tendencies toward evil. This work would complete the work of redemption begun in a person at conversion. Wood defined this experience in general terms.

> When guilt is forgiven in justification, and all pollution is
> removed in entire sanctification, so that grace possesses the
> heart and nothing contrary to grace, then the moral condition
> is reached to which the Scriptures give the name of perfection,
> or entire sanctification.[9]

A book by Mrs. Phoebe Palmer was printed by the Army
and used as another of the primary teaching sources of the
experience of entire sanctification. In this book, Mrs. Palmer
clearly described the goal of this experience.

> "My desire, my all-absorbing desire, is to be literally one
> with God. No desire, no aim, apart from the will of God. All—
> body, soul, and spirit—at the service of God. This is my idea
> of Scriptural Sanctification."[10]

The Salvation Army described this experience in more detail. In writing to the field officer, (F.O.) holiness was presented as a moral experience.

> "Holiness means the wise government of the body. The F.O., as a true successor of St. Paul, will keep his body under—that is, in its proper place—treating it always as a servant, and not as a master."[11]

Holiness was also presented as an ethical experience.

> "Holiness in the F.O. means that he shall be true and honest in word and deed, in all his dealings with his soldiers and superior officers, and with everybody else."[12]

And again:

> "Let no officer, soldier, or anyone . . . , for a moment suppose that there can be any holiness apart from truth, and uprightness, honour, and integrity, between man and man."[13]

Finally, holiness was presented as a spiritual experience. "Holiness in the F.O. means that he shall be fully consecrated to the glory of God and the Salvation of men."[14]

Even as the Army expected its converts to immediately become soul-winners, it expected its converts to immediately pursue the blessings of entire sanctification. Their new conversion experience was the most conducive position from which to launch this quest for wholeness. Wood quoted Wesley on this matter.

> We have not made it a *rule, as soon as ever persons are justified, to remind them of "going on unto perfection."* WHEREAS THIS IS THE VERY TIME PREFERABLE TO ALL OTHERS. They have then the simplicity of little children; and they are fervent in spirit, ready to cut off a right hand or pluck out the right eye. But, if we once suffer this fervour to subside, we shall find it hard enough to bring them again even to this point. [*Letter to Thomas Rankin*.][15]

The doctrine of sanctification argued that in the experience of salvation, the power and purpose of God are such that man could and must have complete, total victory over sin, expressed or hidden. All sin had to go. Holiness was not some additional responsibility or privilege but a necessary ingredient for Christian life. *The Officer* warned:

> Many soldiers imagine, . . . , that if no profession of holiness is made, inconsistency of conduct is justifiable, or if not actually so, is at any rate excusable. It cannot be too clearly enforced that God demands purity of life and a whole-hearted surrender of all we possess, by everyone who professes to be His follower. No circumstance or condition will justify disobedience or wrong-doing, nor relieve anyone from the responsibility of being all that God would have them to be.[16]

This goal is clear and consistent in all Army literature.

For those who accept the assertions of this doctrine of sanctification, the problem comes in the question of the receipt of this blessing. There are those who believe that being justified and regenerated, the believer is sanctified, set apart and purified, from that time on to the point of death. Others believe that subsequent to salvation, in the spiritual development of the new believer, the carnal nature with its evil tendencies is uncovered. At this time, a second divine work of cleansing and surrender is required to replace that carnal nature with a holy nature. The Salvation Army belonged in this second camp.

For those who believe in a second distinct work of grace or a second blessing, there is a further problem. How is this second work of grace accomplished? There is general agreement that it is by faith, but, what is the nature of the faith that sanctifies and what are the implications of that concept of faith?

In its formative years, The Salvation Army ascribed to a kind of leap of faith resting on the promises of the Bible that God would answer all prayers. It believed that God wanted his people pure and holy and that he had promised to make them so if they only believed, asked, and by faith received. In one of the earliest issues of *The Officer*, a kind of "four spiritual laws of sanctification" was discussed. These "laws" were:

1. That we believe in its attainability here and now.

2. Sacrifice being essential that it be real, complete, absolute.

3. The acceptance of the Divine Cleanser and Keeper by the exercise of faith.

4. Resolution to follow Christ and walk in the light of God.[17]

This was a kind of "check-list" approach to a spiritual experience. Answer all the questions "yes" and you may believe that the experience is yours. The emphasis is on God's promise to entirely sanctify and his desire to do it now, if you will only believe. *The Christian Mission Magazine* quoted an Episcopalian on holiness faith. "My prayer is so different from what it was before. I don't ask, expecting an answer at some other time, but I believe *I receive it now, while I am praying*, and the Holy Ghost says, You have it."[18] The writer went on.

> We are not to wait God's time as some say; it is unscriptural. NOW is God's time; we are not to wait for power to believe; this is a dangerous snare of the enemy. If we must wait for power, we cannot believe without it; and consequently, all that do not believe are lost because God did not give the power.[19]

Mrs. Palmer wrote about faith and power:

> "The *faith* SHALL bring the power;" but do not expect to *feel* the power *before* you have exercised the faith. This would be expecting the fruit before the tree is planted; the power to *live* and *dwell* in God comes *through believing.*[20]

The basis for believing is faith in the Word of God, not feelings or power. Wood argued:

> If we would be saved, we must stop *quarreling* with our *feelings* and trust all *now* and *forever* upon the immutable Word of God, and we must have just the right kind and the right amount of feeling. The purest faith is exercised in the absence of all feeling, and we are to take God at His word,

and rely upon His truth, and give it the same confidence as though it were proclaimed from heaven by God Himself in a voice of thunder.[21]

Wood referred to this "pure" faith as "naked" faith and took some exception to Wesley who presented a sanctifying faith of a different nature. Wood quoted Wesley. "'None, therefore, ought to believe that the work is done until there is added the testimony of the Spirit witnessing his entire sanctification as clearly as his justification.'"[22] This was a God-given faith resting on an inner witness of the Spirit. Wood said of Wesley:

> This position of Mr. Wesley is safe, and applicable as a general rule; and yet, perhaps, there may be some exceptions to it, as in those cases where God may be pleased to hold the soul for a season, after the work is done, to a *naked* faith in His word, before the Spirit's witness is given. If we do not mistake, this has been the experience of some of the clearest witnesses of perfect love. Perhaps the same may be true in some cases of justification.[23]

The danger in this position on naked faith is that someone can be encouraged to accept a work of God which is suppose to permeate every aspect of their being without any evidence of it whatsoever, simply on the basis of a desire for it. Wood recognized this dangerous possibility, but argued that not recognizing the blessing when it is there is a greater danger among Christians.

> It may be professed too soon, before it is really attained. In this case, a profession is disastrous both to the confessor and to the cause. But in avoiding this extreme do not run to the other, as, in view of the opposition in the Church to the profession of holiness, there is much danger that you will not profess it soon enough, than that you will profess it too soon.[24]

Wood's argument is contradictory. If naked faith is efficacious, how can one profess it before really attaining the blessing? If naked faith is efficacious it is instrumental, God must honor according to his word and the blessing must be imparted and the life must sooner or later exhibit the fruits of this purifying experience. However, the results of this experience were not so easily attained. This is a dangerous oversimplification of the nature of entire sanctification and the work it is to accomplish in the human life. The purifying of the very essence of being, the fundamental redirecting of the individual's will, demanded an extensive work of God in the deepest recesses of the hearts of individuals who were already believers. In *The Christian Mission Magazine*, this work of God was described.

> The light of God reveals the "hidden things of darkness" pride, self-esteem, self-complacency, love of approbation, disguised in the laudable desire to gain the confidence of others, in order the better to influence them on the side of truth. The Holy Spirit showed the need of an inward crucifixion, bad faith, weak though it was, grasp the two-edged sword, look up for power to use it, and begin its piercing, probing work, seeking out the secret, lurking selfishness of unsatisfied desire, "cutting off the right hand, plucking out the right eye," and severing away every tie which kept the spirit grovelling in the dust, away from its own native element, its nobler sphere of glorious freedom and lofty aspirations . . . .[25]

> Such waiting before the Lord to be washed, cleansed, to be made clean! Such hoping, such looking up and expecting— the door of the heart wide open to receive—until the ever-blessed Jesus took possession of the temple His own precious blood had purified and His Holy Spirit had fitted up! Now, bless His holy name! He reigns there supreme.[26]

Here is pursuit and perseverance in quest of an experience which is to be validated by the testimony of the Holy Spirit in the human life. This preparation is more than simple, naked faith that we have received *something*. Here we wait for God to witness to us that the work is done. Leaping blindly into the dark to accept something about which we have no evidence in our hearts and lives raises the danger of corrupting faith with presumption. Booth, writing in one of the earliest of his publications, *The East London Evangelist*, unconsciously gave a clear picture of the tension between a naked faith that caused God to bestow a blessing and a persevering, soul-searching faith which allowed God to act to prepare one for the blessing. Booth argued that one must offer himself fully, laying aside all sins and any weight that is holding him back, and examine himself in light of his relationship to the Holy Spirit. A complete consecration of body, soul, spirit, and mind must be made to Christ. Then Booth said:

> . . . believe that according to His word He accepts the offering, that the blood cleanses, and the Spirit fills. Claim him with humble boldness as your own. Don't doubt, or fear, or reason; but steadily believe, though the fearful flesh, a lying devil, an infidel world, and cold-hearted professors all suggest that it is impossible that God should, according to his unfailing promise, cleanse you from *all* unrighteousness, and preserve you blameless, and fill you with all the divine fullness. Hold on! Though your feelings are barren, your way dark, and your difficulties be multiplied, steadily hang on to the Word of God. You cannot possibly be wrong here. Keep your offering on the altar. Maintain the truth of God's word; He has spoken and shall it not come to pass? Most assuredly it will. You are His by creation, redemption, and now by covenant. He will surely claim, fill and satisfy His own. If God be not a liar all things are yours; *believe* this, *rest* upon it, and you will soon *feel* it. Remember, the most naked faith is the most efficacious. Expect the baptism every hour; wait if He tarry. "This kind goeth not forth but by prayer and fasting"; and the Lord whom you seek shall suddenly come to his temple.[27]

Practically the entire quote exhorts the reader to exercise naked faith. But the last two sentences recognize that naked faith does not cause God to bestow the blessing of entire sanctification. In the beginning, Booth encourages, "claim, believe, don't doubt," and at the end he says, "hang on if God should tarry." John Fletcher is quoted in the same magazine: "'O, my brothers and sisters, pray, pray for this outpouring of the Spirit! Wrestle, agonize with God till it is given.'"[28] The emphasis is again upon God and his part in bestowing the blessings in his time, not on the basis of naked faith. Booth, writing in *The Officer* some twenty years later, encouraged:

> Even if you are not able right away to testify to the posses-
> sion of a clean heart—if you are only seeking it, 'Blessed are
> they that do hunger and thirst after righteousness,' even
> before they are filled. Oh! There is a wonderful power in the
> tears and prayers and longings of hungering souls; . . .[29]

Booth recognized a place for preparation and perseverance
in the pursuit of holiness, and an acceptance that this blessing was ultimately a blessing God bestowed at his good
pleasure. Even Wood made an allowance on this point.

> . . . although there is a diversity of operation both with
> respect to the *divine* and *human* spirit, yet the blessed results
> are the same. Let us never mark out a way for God, but seek
> the cleansing power of the Holy Ghost, until it comes just as
> He is pleased to manifest it.[30]

The Army in its formative years did not deal with the tension in the concept of sanctifying faith. It emphasized the
immediacy of the blessing and the idea of a faith with
power to appropriate the blessing. It argued that God's
good pleasure was to bestow the blessing *now* if one would
only believe. Wood said: "Am I now committing all, and
trusting in Christ? If you are it is done."[31] Mrs. Palmer gave
an example which emphasized the instrumentality of faith.

> He had sought for this blessing a number of years; but he
> now thought that he would try the Lord at His WORD, and
> see if He would receive him, if he would give himself up in
> this simple way. He formally had thought that it required a
> great effort upon his part; but now he simply paused and sat
> still in his chair, without any distress of mind, or even shed-
> ding a tear, and whispered a simple prayer *in faith*, and the
> blessing was imparted.[32]

Wood held to the immediacy of the experience, even though
the one entirely sanctified might not be conscious of the
instant the gift was bestowed.

> Many who believe in sudden conversions cannot tell the
> precise time of their conversion. They know they are convert-
> ed, . . . but cannot tell the time of the change. The same holds

true in regard to entire sanctification. While most who are in the possession of this grace sought it as an *instantaneous* work, and received it *instantaneously*, others cannot tell the precise time when the full cleansing was wrought; and yet it was wrought in an instant.[33]

Mrs. Palmer also stressed the instantaneous character of the blessing.

It is of great importance that you look at this great Salvation as a *present* Salvation, received momentarily from above. The blood of Jesus *cleanseth*; not that it can or will cleanse at some *future* period, but it *cleanseth now*, while you lay your all upon that "altar that sanctifieth the gift!"[34]

Thus, under the Christian dispensation, the entire sanctification of spirit, soul, and body takes place the moment the entire being is laid believingly *upon* the Christian altar. And when the entire being touches Christ, that moment it is holy. For "whatsoever toucheth the altar shall be holy."[35]

Bramwell Booth illustrated the Army's position metaphorically.

It was only for converted people, they would receive it in a moment and receive it by faith. As one would cash a cheque at the bank on *presenting* it, so believing for this word of purity, was the presenting to Him of His promise and the *claiming* of the gift. The cheque might be right. The bank might be right. But if it was not presented it could do no good, and be no use to the pauper who carried it in his pocket. He would be a pauper still. We must trust and try God at once.[36]

Later, as General, Bramwell is quoted regarding this second blessing.

I only make one further remark, and that is this: If ever you are to live that life it must have a beginning: it must begin at some time. There must be a moment, just as that moment came to Jesus Christ, and just as it has come to all who have entered into deliverance from evil in this life of power over temptation—there must come a moment when you say finally, when you fix it, when it is done, not my will, but Thine be done![37]

. . . I feel that tonight some of you who have never yet entered into that Full Salvation . . . this is an opportunity God has given you of coming away from the other life: and this is the place and hour it can be done. This can be the place when you can begin that life of Full Deliverance.[38]

While the Army accepted a second definite work of grace accomplished at a specific crisis point, it made a place for process. Process with respect to entire sanctification was seen in the approach to the blessing as asserted by Wood above: "The approach to entire sanctification may be gradual."[39] The early Army also acknowledged and accepted process *in* entire sanctification, subsequent to the crisis experience. In fact, the Army was quite concerned that progress in entire sanctification took place.

> Now the lives of some of our dear Soldiers show . . . , few signs of growth in Holiness. They are still in the infancy of a holy life when they should be progressing toward the full stature of men in Christ Jesus. They show comparatively little knowledge of the deeper things of the life of love.[40]

As in the doctrine of salvation, so in the doctrine of sanctification, the experience was to result in real change. What may have started out as a blind leap into the dark was expected to become a knowledgeable faith resting on an inner assurance that the blessing had been received. In the doctrine book of 1881, the question was asked whether a soul could believe that the blessing was given immediately on the basis of this faith.

> Yes, *always*—that is, if a soul, having the assurance that he does fully renounce all known and doubtful wrong doing, and gives himself up to the will of God in all things, thus *trusts* God for *full* cleansing, he has the authority of God's Word for believing that the work is done, *no matter how he feels*; and he must hold on to this faith until the feeling comes.[41]

What is important here is that the Army insisted that a feeling of assurance be expected and experienced. Again from the 1881 doctrine book:

> Sometimes, God tries faith for a little time, and, although the soul has the witness that he has put his sacrifice on the

altar—that he is fully consecrated, and has the witness in himself that he believes that God accepts it; still, he may have, like Abraham of old, *to wait* for the fire, which not only makes him inwardly *feel* and *know* that God cleanses his soul, but, if he *watches* his sacrifice, and *waits* a season, the fire will *assuredly* come.[42]

Mrs. Palmer asserted that "true faith will produce *feeling*, but it may at first be little other than solid satisfaction, arising from an implicit reliance on God."[43] General Bramwell Booth wrote:

> . . . it is our privilege, your privilege, my privilege, to know where we stand before God, and be able to say to Him, 'I know in whom I have believed'; and be able to say for ourselves that that holy assurance that the Spirit alone can give, it is mine . . .[44]

However, ". . . sometimes, He keeps His people waiting for that feeling of confirmation of their acceptance, and of their sanctified experience."[45]

> ". . . I do not say that the assurances of His favour are always given to us at the moment of our asking, but I do say that there will be a moment when that assurance will come in answer to faith."[46]

While Bramwell recognized that this assurance came from God in his own time, in true Army fashion he encouraged people to look for the assurance immediately.

> Some of you will perhaps say to me, 'In what direction may I especially look for that assurance?' Look for it this afternoon—now! Your acceptance is not something in the past, but something in the present—knowing you have the presence of God, and have the witness of His spirit—being without doubt about it.[47]

> This afternoon if you have not already done it, ask God to give you that living conscious knowledge of your acceptance with Him; that you are His child, His servant, making Himself known to you as your Saviour, and that assurance is just as truly promised for that work of sanctifying grace which He has promised.[48]

Then it is His great joy to say it is so. You will know that it
is so. The Holy Spirit will give you that conscious certainty
about which there can be no doubt. If it is so with you, all is
well. If it is not so, why should it not be here this afternoon.[49]

The need for divine assurance or the "witness of the
Spirit" that the work of entire sanctification was accomplished was very mystical in nature. But, characteristic of
Salvation Army thought, there was something very practical to undergird the more mystical. Full surrender or total
commitment were foundation blocks on which even faith
rested, as well as assurance. In the words of Rev. Wood:

Salvation is by appropriating faith, and such faith or trust
can be exercised only when there is—consciousness of complete surrender to God. A justified state can exist only in connection with a serious, honest intention to obey all the commands of God.[50]

Palmer wrote:

Though the blessing is received through faith, and not by
the works of the law, yet it is impossible to exercise that faith
which brings the blessing, until we are willing to bring the
sacrifice of the body, soul, and spirit, and leave it there.[51]

The doctrine book of 1881 instructed:

He must give up being his *own master*, and living to please
and profit *himself*, and go back to God with *all He possesses*,
much or little, and lay *himself* at Jehovah's feet, and offer to
live *wholly* to please and profit Him.[52]

Wood put this total commitment in its place in the process
of God's sanctifying work.

Submission to God, or entire consecration, *is our act*, with
assisting grace. Entire sanctification *is God's work* wrought in
the soul. . . Sanctification always includes consecration; but
entire consecration does not necessarily include entire sanctification—it *precedes* and *accompanies it*.[53]

The doctrine book of 1881 stated this about the consecration
necessary for entire sanctification:

> This, it will be perceived, if a reality, is no *easy* task, and can only be done in the might of the Holy Ghost; but, when it is done, when all is laid on the altar—body, soul, spirit, goods, reputation, *all[,] all, all*—then the fire descends, and burns up all the dross and defilement, and fills the soul with burning zeal and love and power.[54]

This was the kind of practical consideration and requirement that kept the Army's feet firmly planted on the ground in the midst of the turmoil of life. The Salvation Army did not allow its soldiers to get caught up in any kind of wishful thinking mentality which accepted something vague.

For those who had difficulty accepting the blessing of entire sanctification, the Army provided very practical advice for the continual pursuit of the blessing. Colonel Nicol wrote:

> . . . to meet this difficulty, that the officer during the day should, come when possible, get those together who come forward in the morning and have a meeting with them alone, when they should give their testimony as to their difficulties and also say what God has called them to do. The officer would thus know their spiritual condition and would at once be able to appoint them to some definable work, also urge them and help them in the fulfillment of their consecration vows.[55]

Regarding those who continually came forward for holiness, Colonel Nicol added that the officer must

> . . . get to know what is their peculiar difficulties, and take the trouble to teach and advise them what to do, and in this way be the means of getting them right and turning their earnestness into a channel that could be of service to the corps.[56]

This sober, persistent quest for something practical and definite kept the doctrine of entire sanctification from becoming an excursion into a world of mystical sensationalism. The Army preached a conscious experience. The public testimony to this experience, expected by the Army, demanded one to come to grips with what was happening in his life. Quoting James Caughey, Wood wrote: "'The more frequently I spoke of this great blessing, confessing it, and urging others to press after it, the *clearer* my evidence became.'"[57]

Entire sanctification was preached as a real experience that evidenced a real change. As such, public testimony was absolutely appropriate. A lady conscious of the sin remaining in her heart after being saved, experienced a further work of God and testified "'... from that hour I have felt no anger, no pride, no wrong temper of any kind; nothing contrary to the pure love of God, which I feel continually.'"[58] Wood quoted Dr. Adam Clarke on this point.

> Soon after this, while earnestly wrestling with the Lord in prayer, and endeavouring self-desperately to believe, *I found a change wrought in my soul,* which I endeavoured, through grace, to maintain amid the grievous temptations and accusations of the subtle foe.[59]

The Army's position on entire sanctification brought forth the same opposing arguments that Wesley and the holiness movement had encountered. Critics saw in the Army's doctrine a denial of any kind of remaining sin so that sin was no longer a threat. It was argued that the person who claimed entire sanctification as preached by the Army tended not to recognize the deeper, more subtle forms of sin in the nature of man. One concerned writer warned:

> "It is not til sooner or later some awful fall startles and horrifies the Church of God that honest souls begin to tremble and to examine where they stand. Was it after all the truth of God, or the devil's lie?"[60]

The Church of the nineteenth century had a healthy respect for the sinfulness of man. Even among those denying original sin and eternal punishment, the sin of man was never repudiated. In most circles of the established Church, the claims of the Army's soldiers to be entirely sanctified, especially since they were people of the most common classes, seemed shocking and presumptuous. *The Church Quarterly Review,* covering an Army service, reported: "One after another, the speakers, men and women, stand up and give their 'experience' of receiving what they call 'the second blessing,' or sanctification."[61]

> Sanctification, according to this teaching, is not a progressive development of the justified soul in a course of vigilance, humility, and faith, but a gift to be received in a second, putting the whole man at once on a higher level of life than in the days when he was only "saved."[62]

This critic saw self-conceit as the great error in the Army's position. Canon Farrar, one of the most respected churchmen of Victorian England, was another critic.

> . . . I would ask them how they can expect that ignorance should not be accompanied by egotism and self-assurance when they put forward men and women on platforms before thousands of people to claim sanctification as the result of sudden conversion in that deplorable proceeding which they call "The Exhibition of Trophies," and, which seems even more shocking, "The Exhibition of Hallelujah Lasses"?[63]

Not only was the doctrine of entire sanctification as a second work of grace called into question, but its idea of instantaneous bestowal was appalling to Farrar, who argued:

> "The best and truest saints of God in all ages have felt that sanctification is a gradual gift which can only be slowly and laboriously, and, at the best, most imperfectly attained."[64]

For Farrar, the true test of God's children

> . . . does lie in the humble, continuous fulfillment of daily duties, in daily prayer for daily forgiveness, in the daily cleansing of daily assoilments, in the use of God's sacraments and appointed means of grace, in bringing forth the fruits of the Spirit, of which deep humility and holy charity are among the greatest and the best.[65]

The Army did not preach a sinless perfection anymore than had Wesley. In the mission magazine predating The Salvation Army, an article on sanctification testified: "I never look at my imperfections and short-comings without believing that His blood does *that moment* wash them all away."[66] The Army was very much aware of what Wesley called the "infirmities of the flesh" with which man was bound until the day of resurrection and eternal life. The doctrine book of 1881 argued that imperfect people could not perfectly obey the perfect law of God.[67] Further, the entirely sanctified were never free from temptation, mistakes in judgment, or bodily and mental infirmities.[68] But, in the area of will, of intention, of attitude, the Army believed that Christ, his love and righteousness could and would reign, negating the power of sin to bring rebellion against God.

This idea of divine intention and power was large in scope. It portrayed a salvation that culminated in saintliness and purity. Entire sanctification was an experience aimed like an arrow at the innermost recesses of the heart, at the understanding of self, motives, aspirations, duties, and responsibilities. Here the Army went beyond superficial feelings or intellectual assent to the "resolve-of-will." Here was a quest for essential change, new creation. This serious, deep penetration into the being of a person gave substance and stability to the movement. Railton recognized this when he wrote regarding prayer and holiness:

> To these Nights of Prayer perhaps more than anything else we owe that perfect unity of teaching and of aim as to holy living which is so vital to our existence. If the Army were to develop an enthusiasm not fully directed towards holiness and righteousness of life, it would be sadly in danger of becoming either fanatical on the one hand, or worldly on the other.[69]

> The spiritual children of the Army have been taught to trace every evil thought and word and deed back to the innate corruption of the heart, and to pray in faith for the instant removal of these inward roots of bitterness, which, springing up, have troubled them.[70]

The experience of entire sanctification was absolutely indispensable for the spiritual well-being of any and all Christians. But, for the Army, this experience was not an end in itself.

Victory over sin in the very nature of man would produce believers who were more than conquerors over the powers and principalities of darkness. These believers would be prepared to do good works.

> The true Salvationist believes in being good. He knows no real ground for concluding that his religion will be of any value either in this life or the life to come, unless it produces holiness of heart and life. To him, faith without works is dead, corrupt, injurious, a mockery, a delusion and a snare. While his every hope of meritorious consideration hangs solely on the sacrifice of Jesus Christ, he believes that such reliance, if genuine will be evidenced by a corresponding life of pureness and love.[71]

In these early years, the Army never considered purity apart from consecration to God. Wood exhorted: "Search and surrender, and research and surrender again, until you get every vestige of self upon the altar of consecration."[72] Palmer said:

> GOSPEL holiness is that *state* which is attained by the believer when, through *faith* in the infinite merit of the Saviour, body and soul, with every ransomed faculty, are ceaselessly presented, a living sacrifice, to God; . . .[73]

While Mrs. Palmer referred to this experience as a "state," it was not to be understood as a once-for-all experience. There is an existential element that makes it a living experience offering continual consecration.

> . . . "sanctification," as applied to believers, comprehends inconceivably greater blessedness than a mere nominal setting apart of body and soul, with every power to God. The sacrifice, or service, however well intended, could not for a moment be acceptable without the washing of regeneration, and the renewing of the Holy Ghost. And then, in order to be continually washed, cleansed, and renewed after the image of God, the sacrifice must be *ceaselessly* presented.[74]

Instead of a danger toward self-conceit, this position encouraged continued humility in the progress of the holy life. Again quoting Palmer: ". . . the blessing of entire sanctification cannot be understandingly retained otherwise than by the most careful circumspection in *all things*."[75] The doctrine book of 1881 tied together the concepts of holiness and service. It declared that "sanctification is the separation of the soul from sin, and the devotion of the whole being to the will and service of God."[76] It is ". . . *complete deliverance* from sin. Sin is *destroyed* out of the soul, and all the powers, faculties, possessions, and influences of the soul are given up to the service and glory of God."[77] *The Times* of London, reporting on The Salvation Army, picked up this connection between holiness and service within the context of holiness theology.

> The two earlier meetings were "holiness councils," when the members and followers of the army were instructed in the offices of the Holy Spirit and encouraged to give up the world in act and not merely in theory, and to devote themselves more wholly to the Master's service.[78]

The Army's holiness theology was directly applicable to its mission. It was not a contemplative doctrine analyzed to develop theological discourses on purity and total surrender. It was rather an active, dynamic doctrine calling forth saintly people for God-ordained purposes. As we have already found, the ultimate service for the Master was soul-winning. In this mission the Army's holiness theology was not only active but vital, an emphasis from early mission days. Booth himself had written in *The East London Evangelist:*

> I would not have you think that I imagine for a moment that you have not the Spirit. By your fruits I know you. No men could do the works that are being done in your midst, except God was with them. All glory to Jesus, He is enabling you to give proof of your heavenly calling. But how much more might be done had you *all* received this pentecostal baptism *in all its fullness?* If every soul were inflamed, and every lip touched, and every mind illuminated, and every heart purified with a hallowed flame?[79]

Booth concluded:

> The whole city would feel it. God's people in every direction would catch fire, and the sinners would fall on every side. Difficulties would vanish, devils be conquered, infidels believe, and the glory of God be displayed. As it is written, every valley would be filled, and every mountain and hill be brought low, and the crooked would be made straight, and the rough ways be made smooth, and all flesh would see the salvation of God.[80]

In entire sanctification, the experience of salvation was understood to reach down to the deepest recesses of human nature affecting the very will of man. At this point, complete victory over willful sin was mandated. This complete victory was a necessary requisite in the salvation war to which the Army was called. It was this experience by which divine power in generous amount was made available to God's soldiers as they labored with him to reach the lost.

Chapter VIII

God and Man: Beginning of Church or Movement?

I n the beginning years of The Salvation Army, the Army had no formal doctrine of the Church. In fact, the Army endeavored in every way to avoid any sectarian or denominational tags. How is it then that we can even consider a doctrine of the Church?

To some extent, this doctrine is implied in the theological constructs of the early Army; namely, its doctrines of salvation and sanctification. In these doctrines, we find a theology of reconciliation, faith, and mission. This theology of relationship between God and man is central to a concept of the Church. Many of the disfranchised of Victorian England found a place where they belonged. It was a place where God was encouragingly near. God was real, consciously present, accessible, and personally interested in every individual. However, this relationship was quite different from that perceived by the mainline churches of the day, and it led to something other than a church.

The Victorian period was not a time when metaphysical relationships were popularly emphasized except in the most rational terms. God was acknowledged, but to a certain extent he was removed from creation. He had done his work and done it well. Man possessed in his God-given intelligence that which was necessary to shape a better life. God was on the throne to be worshipped and honored. Man was to do this by his church attendance and his moral and ethical behavior. In the various social and religious movements concerned with the poor all emphasized moral and ethical behavior and encouraged intellectual and cultural development.

The Settlement Movement of the 1870s and 1880s is one of the clearest examples of this popular emphasis directed at the lower classes. It was a movement of intellectuals and university students, which emphasized culture and learning. In 1882, Woods wrote:

> One cannot but be impressed with the fact that the English working men live a more rounded and developed life than the American, comparing grade with grade. No small proportion of them have an intelligent interest in the political questions of the day. They are learning to appreciate the healthful pleasures of social life. They are beginning to care for a knowledge of history and literature. Of course, there are merely suggestions of such a tendency among unskilled labourers; and it is not strongly marked even among the artisans. But one never goes far among English working men without finding signs of this very hopeful influence.[1]

The Settlement Movement endeavored to arouse among the poor an interest in these values and priorities. To do this it tried to transplant the university directly into the slum. The residents of the Toynbee Settlement ". . . dreamed of Toynbee Hall as the nucleus of an East End University. . . ."[2] Their effort was to confront a heathen culture with the university culture.

> . . . it was at Oxford first that the feeling of humanity urged men to go and make their homes in the city of social exiles at the East End of London, living there the life they had learned to live under the influence of the University.[3]

In this university context, while popular education was

offered, even more did the Settlement try to introduce a new cultural expression. Picht asserted that the Settlement ". . . becomes a reservoir of experiences, and it combines elasticity with stability and duration. The individual has every chance for development; . . ."[4]

Some settlements were religiously based. The theology of the Settlement Movement was given in the opening address of University Hall. It was an optimistic approach to the problem of the masses that focused upon the natural rather than the supernatural.

> . . . the ways of God to man and to the world, whatever may still be the darkness and mystery of life, may now—apart from any belief in miraculous events, or localised revelation—be justified by the pondering heart and instructed mind with greater fullness, a livelier spring of hope, and a more reasonable self-devotion, than at any earlier time in the world's history.[5]

A middle-of-the-road of reason and faith was pursued between the end points of a theological spectrum of the nineteenth century; blind faith versus unbelief. These end points are illustrated in references to the Bible.

> Either a magic virtue is still given to it, and it remains a book of riddles and marvels, out of relation to all that an enlarged knowledge of the world can tell us about God and man; or it is impatiently and ignorantly cast aside as having no longer any positive and practical value for us and for our lives.[6]

Reason was the appropriate tool to uncover "whatever may still be the darkness and mystery of life." The difficulty could be resolved through careful observation and analysis. The great need of the day was for a reasoned faith rather than a faith in that which transcended reason.

> It is in the bringing back of *faith*—not the faith which confuses legend with history, or puts authority in the place of knowledge, but the faith which springs from moral and spiritual fact, and may be day after day, and hour after hour, again verified by fact—that the great task of our generation lies.[7]

In the religious settlements reasoned faith was to be accompanied by good works patterned after Christ who went to the people to teach them by word and example.

> It was not enough to *preach* the Gospel, it must be *lived* within sight of the people. Religion is life more than Doctrine; its expression demands something broader than mere words, and we therefore turn to consider the Settlement Movement as the expression of the Spirit of Jesus Christ along a line especially congenial to the heart and mind of youth.[8]

In the program at Oxford House, an explicitly Christian-based settlement, life in all of its cultural dimensions was emphasized.

> The Oxford House men give valuable assistance in the ordinary parish work of their district. They visit regularly two wards of the London Hospital, nearby. In the summer, they meet the agnostic lectures on their own ground by preaching in the open air. They assist clergymen in carrying on missions.[9]

> The Oxford House is the centre of a Federation of Working Men's clubs, all of which refrain from selling intoxicants, and most of which are connected with churches and missions. There are thirty-five clubs in this Federation, representing four thousand members. Through the Federation, competitions in music and athletics are arranged, lectures provided, excursions taken, and joint committees are formed for discussing and acting upon whatever sanitary, municipal, and industrial questions are most important at the time.[10]

On Sunday afternoon a lecture might be presented on religious, social, or literary subjects. The evening service was conducted as a mission meeting with traditional preaching.[11] However, the emphasis was upon moral and ethical behavior as well as religious respectability.

Toynbee Hall was not a religious settlement. It was primarily an institution of cultural education supported by the universities of Oxford and Cambridge, the "Universities' Settlement Association," and generous friends. It focused upon the workers in the East End of London, particularly those who wanted to rise up out of their poverty and social circumstances.[12] Inglis asserted that "Toynbee Hall's religion was syncretic, undogmatic and humanitarian."[13] This was one of the settlements that consciously emphasized moral and ethical concerns in lieu of the spiritual.

> It is obvious that there is a strong craving in modern and restless society for some sensuous arrangement of worship— some beautiful and satisfying expression of religious feeling. I fear that a careful observer will also note that in this there is but a faint effect on the activities of real life; emotion devours itself.[14]

"Our best chance with him lies in practical appeals to him for moral betterment."[15]

The Settlement Movement tried to develop comradeship between the settlers and those they came to assist.

> . . . condescension was ruled out, and comradship took its place. Where a deep religious spirit found clothing in the Settlement idea, compassion—[a] peculiarly Christian word in its deepest significance—awoke and became active.[16]

"The central and deep thing . . . in the whole Settlement Movement is the place it gives to *Friendship*."[17]

> . . . because friendship was the greatest enrichment of life to those who lived in a University together and made and won friends there, they naturally turned in that direction to express their religious life on a broader field.[18]

Though much was made of communication and comradery, class distinctions were accepted. The distance between classes was the cause of concern, not the existence of class distinctions. Rev. Brooke asserted:

> "The gap between classes . . . yawned dangerously wide now, and could be closed only if members of the educated classes went among the poor and helped them back to humanity...."[19]

Inglis discussed this emphasis in the views of another settlement founder, Mr. Samuel Barnett.

As a member of the Church of England he wanted to see people adopt certain principles, but as an Englishman he wished above all to see the islands of class joined by bridges of goodwill. The Settlement, he believed was a better base than the mission on which to build such bridges.[20]

> The settler comes to the poor as man to man in the conviction that it means a misfortune for all parties and a danger for the nation, if the different classes live in complete isolation of thought and environment. He comes to bridge the gulf between the classes.[21]

The settlement idea went back to an earlier culture, not organized horizontally in classes but vertically in terms of responsibilities and obligations where duty was the primary value. It reaffirmed the duty of the rich to the poor. The intellectuals endeavored to pull society back together into the ordered world of the eighteenth century. A report on the Toynbee project declared:

> The university settlements are a stern rebuke to the wealthy families and churches moving farther and farther into aristocratic quarters, and leaving slums in their wake as they go. The Settlements suggest that this tendency is hurtful to the rich as well as to the poor.[22]

The intellectuals believed

> . . . that "those who have" owe something to "those who have not," and that the more their service costs them the more it is worth to the community. They offer friendship; and teaching of Jesus is clear and definite—that friendship is the richest and most enriching thing in human life.[23]

Picht identified the Settlement Movement's emphasis on duty.

> Its guiding star was the feeling of its pioneers that a sacrifice of love was necessary in order to make up to their brothers, who lay in economic serfdom, for the centuries of forgotten duty on the part of those who held in their hands culture and power.[24]

The Picht report drew an early conclusion regarding the Settlement and the Army.

> General Booth, the founder of the Salvation Army, cries out at the end of a life blessed with unheard of success: "I have sought all my life to reach with one hand the rich, and with the other the poor, and have not been able to." The Settlement Movement has succeeded in doing so. It has built bridges which can never be broken down. It has been one of the strongest and most successful forces in the struggle for the unity of the nation.[25]

This assertion was premature. The possibility of a bridge existed, but a bridge serves little purpose if few people use it, and the poor had little use for the idea of a slum university.

A Rev. Rooper, writing on Booth and the Army, referred to this settlement philosophy and pronounced his own judgment, shared by others.

> . . . in our luxurious age it had come to be thought a great thing for some of the more or less well endowed with this world's goods to leave their comfortable homes and pass a few hours in instructing, consoling, and assisting with alms, the distressed, and too often sin-burthened. All honour to their motives, but the gulf between them and those whose condition, spiritually and physically, they would raise, is too deep to be bridged over by such means.[26]

To those dying of starvation and filled with the frustration of being "left out," the idea of studying for a year or so in order to "move up" was not a bright prospect. Many could not wait a year or two for progress. Others had neither the patience nor the stomach for study. The desperately poor found little interest in this movement, and it became less and less effective.

The settlers were considered by many to be intruders into the neighborhoods of the poor. A missioner was expected to intrude but not the secular man. Also, the Settlement introduced artificial conditions foreign to the neighborhoods separating the settlers from the poor.[27] Finally, the settlement idea itself came into question.

> It is held that the organism of society has to-day become so

complicated that the demand expressed in the Parable of the Good Samaritan to help one's neighbour can find its application in this shape only to members of one's own class, and nothing is to be done for the rest but to improve the social and economic mechanism; that is to say, a radical change of front, by which the Movement is placed in opposition to itself.[28]

The bridge to the poor was not being built. Picht uncovered a problem in the nature of the settlers themselves.

> ... the settlers are no Franciscans, but on an average nothing more nor less than loveable, healthy, prosperous young Englishmen, with good hearts, in whom during the daytime, in their profession, one sees nothing remarkable to distinguish them from others of their kind.[29]

"The greatness and the tragedy of the Movement lie in this that it has undertaken to place men of the world in the service of a work to which they are not equal."[30] The weakness in the settlement idea, reported Picht,

> ... rests on the mistaken idea that a number of well-meaning cultured people could become neighbours to the poor whenever they chose. This is possible so long as they are carried over all hindrances by a wave of enthusiasm, or so far as their life is filled with living Christianity; for both can overcome all human obstacles, and it is there that the difficulty lies.[31]

The Settlement had the ingredients of a grand idea but never became an effective scheme. It was noble only to a few who were momentarily moved by this concept. The idea needed to be clothed in the lives of a kind of people it did not produce. A new people were called for but never found. The Army consciously opposed settlement philosophy. Inglis uncovered this fundamental disagreement.

> To William Booth and his followers the ideas and the strategy of people like Samuel Barnett appeared mistaken. The attempt to bring the culture of the educated classes to the poor seemed to them a misreading of God's will. Booth's wife Catherine remarked in her last address that Christ came to save the world, not to civilize it; and she said of those people who put any hope in education: "you cannot reform man

morally by his intellect; this is the mistake of most social reformers. You must reform man by his SOUL!"[32]

The Army steadfastly maintained that the problem was one of human depravity. People needed to be saved, and this was God's personal work accomplished by him and those he called into his service. The focus was upon God and his people, God and man in cooperative union.

> Oh, may the Holy Ghost, whose office has been practically ignored, and whose power has been shut out by the great mass of professing Christians, open their eyes to see that the reason the world is not long ago at the feet of Jesus is because they have tried to do the work in the power of the flesh, by educating and apologising and arguing with the intellect, and forgetting that it is by the foolishness of prophecy and the power of God that it pleases Him to save souls.[33]

The Army brought God and Man together in a most dynamic relationship as co-workers in the effort to save the lost and perfect the saved. Booth testified:

> . . . the business of my life has been not only to make a holy character but to live a life of loving activity in the service of God and man. I have ever felt that true religion consists not only in being holy myself, but in assisting my Crucified Lord in His work of saving men and women, making them into His Soldiers, keeping them faithful to death, and so getting them into heaven.[34]

Booth's son Bramwell echoed this same concept of cooperation between God and man. He wrote: ". . . one of my favorite texts in the Bible is about 'working together with God,' being 'labourers together with God', . . ."[35] He wrote again:

> I have been so bowed down and overcome with the thought that God condescends to ask us to work with Him for the Salvation of the people around us. But how much more wonderful it is that He should ask us to come and work with Him in doing those things which are needed in ourselves.[36]

The early Army considered God to be clearly transcendent and absolutely sovereign, but allowed this in no way to minimize the significance of man. God's sovereignty was understood to mean that one day he would judge the quick and the dead and man would have to accept his decision as to eternal happiness or endless punishment. However, the Army recognized no divine determination up to this final day. The free will of man was accepted and considered to have a determinative effect upon God's program in this world.

Man was significant both in his utter depravity and in his glorious redemption. At either end of the spectrum, he influenced the world for good or ill. The doctrine book of 1881 inferred this significance of man.

> We know He hates sin, and we believe that He is doing His utmost to get people saved from committing it; and we know also that He fails because He has such a wretched, cowardly set of Soldiers to fight for Him. With true Soldiers, and plenty of them, we have every reason to conclude that He would soon drive sin and the devil out of the world. Let us help Him.[37]

The thought that God "fails" would be enough to arouse the polemic of both Arminian and Calvinist. Could it be that God really needed man to accomplish his plan of salvation in his war against evil? The Army argued yes. General Bramwell Booth wrote:

> . . . He not only says, "Come and love Me because I need your love, and your sympathy," but He says, "Come and help Me, because I need that strength which you can bring, whether it be much or little, to aid Me in the great battle which I am waging."[38]

When the Army asserted the significance of man, it meant the whole of mankind. In this Army, there was a place of importance for children. After all, children needed to be saved as much as adults. Railton pointed out:

> THE GENERAL'S own personal experience, as well as numberless instances that came under his observation in his own and other families, gave him the same assurance as to the need and possibility of the Salvation of children as he had with regard to adults.[39]

Instructions to the Army's Company Guards (Sunday school teachers) emphasized the importance of the conversion of children.

> Again, while endeavouring to instruct and strengthen the young minds with the truths, lessons, and actual Words of the Bible, let us not forget that this alone is not enough. Our aim is before all things and let us never lose sight of it—to win the children for Christ and righteousness.[40]

> Guards, who make not progress themselves in learning how best to arouse the children to alarm and concern about their souls, and about the souls of those around them, can never be really fit to take any Company.[41]

The Army's principles of youth work underscored the importance of children and their conversion.

> 1. We allow none to teach but those who have given evidence that they are truly converted, and are seeking to serve and please God.

> 2. We aim at the definite conversion of every child, and the training of all the children under our care to be true soldiers of the Cross.

> We rely upon the guidance of the Holy Spirit and the Word of God; for conversion is a divine work.[42]

Here was as "real" a conversion as that expected of adults and one in which divine assurance was a must. This is evident in the testimonies of children, printed in the *Little Soldier*.

> "I HAVE been converted three weeks and I have not been so happy in all my life before, and we have such happy times on Saturday afternoon; and this is my experience: 'Since Jesus is mine I will not fear undressing, But gladly put off these garments of clay; to die in the Lord is a covenant blessing, since Jesus to glory through death leads the way.' Thank God that I am still saved, and I mean to go on by God's help." [HAPPY AGNES, aged eleven years.][43]

> "I DO thank God because I am still trusting in His precious blood, I mean to love my Jesus. Amen." [GEORGE, the "CONVERTED LIAR," aged thirteen years.][44]

Many people argued that children could not know the seriousness of conversion, much less possess the assurance of that salvation. They argued that children needed to be taught the basics of education. Spirituality should wait for later years. Sunday schools were conducted not to teach the Bible and the Christian life, but to teach reading, writing, and arithmetic. The Army found great opposition to its ideas regarding children. Railton believed that this was the most difficult of all Booth's revolutionary programs.

> . . . the spectre of the Sunday School ever and anon rises to threaten with a peaceful death, this Divine undertaking. Only the most persistant watchfulness can prevent the narrow idea of instruction, and unbelief as to children's Salvation which is its foundation, from gaining the upper hand. It is so easy to get a thousand children drilled into pretty attention, pretty performances, pretty recitations and singing, and even into some degree of knowledge of the killing letter, but so hard to get any one child really to submit to the one great Teacher of mankind, and be saved![45]

While difficult, this ministry of conversion was absolutely essential. It was necessary not as an end in itself, but because the Army believed children could be soul-winners in their youth.

> . . . we aim also at glorious results in the homes and families which they represent. Rightly taught, each Junior should become a messenger of Salvation in his own home and surroundings, however dark or ignorant these may be.[46]

Railton, a few years later, wrote:

> . . . The General's theory has been proved, on trial, to result in producing heros and heroins, capable, almost in infancy, of daring Battle for God, and becoming, before they reach their majority, thoroughly experienced and intelligent conquerors.[47]

The Army believed that the best prospects to ensure its future lay in the cultivation of its own young people.

> . . . we desire nothing less than to raise up in every part of the world where our Flag is flying centres of teaching, training, and character-making. Little nursery-gardens, so to speak,

devoted to the planting and culture of "trees of righteousness," under the constant direction and inspiration of the Holy Spirit.[48]

. . . the results we desire are not merely to teach, train, and make character among our Juniors alone; but we aim also at producing as a result of our Young People's Work, men and women on fire for souls, and with intelligence, experience, and a zeal in winning them; it is from our Young People's War that we should confidently turn, and not in vain, for our best Officers in the future.[49]

Thus when we, the officers of today, are gone to our reward, these shall push forward with their General's motto impressed upon their hearts and always upon their lips, 'The world for Christ,' and shall win it, laying it as a trophy at the feet of Him who died, while we join in the triumphs of the conquest and share in the spoils.[50]

A youth department was organized to establish a youth army on much the same basis as the adult army. The goal was awesome.

To raise and maintain a force of children who shall not only live godly from day to day, but shall carry on for their King a warfare as continual and as desperate as that of the adult Salvation Soldier, is indeed a stupendous undertaking, but it is to this and nothing less that we have applied ourselves in downright earnest for the last twelve months, and we think we can show that we have already attained an astonishing amount of success.[51]

The Army brought its young people into the spotlight and laid squarely upon their shoulders the challenge of worldwide evangelism, so convinced was it of the power of God's salvation even in the lives of the young.

The Salvation Army laughs at the devil and the assertion that young blood will have its way of worldly pleasures and youthful lusts. Its battle cry, 'The World for God!' includes the children and the spring of man and womanhood. Middle age and hoary head find a place and welcome in the ranks; but to the adversary it opposes a fighting force of those he has been accustomed to consider his own prey—the young. No body of religionists existing offers such a career of work, success, and happiness to saved youth, as The Army.[52]

Another conviction, far ahead of its time, illustrated the
Army's view of the significance of mankind. That conviction
was that women were also called to this ministry of
redemption, not only as soldiers, but also as officers
(ordained clergy). The Army did not deny differences
between the sexes. Women were still considered to be the
weaker sex. The marvel was that God empowered them to
do such great works. Railton reported:

> . . . nothing has more contributed to the success of our
> work in a country where women have been so largely
> repressed, as the fact that The Army has thus demonstrated its
> confidence in God's power to lift up the weakest to the utter-
> most degree.[53]

The role of caring especially belonged to women.

> Oh! should the hearts that are most tender turn away from
> a dying world because it is not thought proper to save them in
> God's appointed way by preaching? Oh! should the gentle,
> loving voices, that first spoke of Jesus to all these multitudes
> in their early days, be silent while, in mature years, they rush
> down to perdition? Oh! should those whose mission it is con-
> fessedly to minister to the ease, the rest, the comfort of man
> look after the *animal*, and leave the soul to be ministered to by
> men—or by nobody, if men's ministrations are not listened
> to? God forbid! He does forbid! 'Let not, man prevail!' 'We
> ought to obey God rather than men!'[54]

However, the pulpit was also recognized as a rightful place
of ministry for women. The requisite was the same as for
men, a divine call.

> If the conviction that God authorises and commands her to
> speak is sufficient, very good; that is all we ask. We want
> nobody, male or female, to do any ordinary preaching. We
> only wish people to speak when and as they are moved by
> the Holy Ghost, for only such speaking can break sinners'
> hearts, and lead them to the Lamb of God.[55]

The early Army did not find God's power, dignity, and
majesty threatened by his appeal to women, but rather
enhanced. It believed that God's willingness to use children

and women brought into focus a bigger God than the one enjoyed by the established churches of the day.

The significance of man is further underlined in the position the Army took with respect to the most depraved. For the Army, not only did redemption of the sinful nature bespeak the power of God, even more so did the redemption of the lowest of the low. When the lowest of the low experienced a new creation and expressed it in holiness and joy, people took notice. Here was real power. Bairstow argued that

> . . . when the musicians can blow out salvation from their own saved and cleansed mouths, and the drummers drum it, and the Miriams timbrel it with arms and hands equally well saved, then the work of winning the soul is often half done before the Gospel is preached.[56]

The Army believed that God's way still included calling into his service fishermen, prostitutes, and tax collectors. In discussing the past and the present, Bramwell Booth recalled:

> 'Fifty-two years ago last month, . . . William Booth broke with many of the traditions of his own life as well as with much that was very sacred and desirable in the religious life of his day, and started out on what must have appeared to many thoughtful people to be a forlorn hope indeed. He had many friends; *but he longed after the enemies of his lord.*[57]

The Salvation Army remained true to this objective. Nothing over-shadowed its special mission to the lowest of the low. Railton quoted from Booth's message to the Wesleyan Methodist Conference of the United Kingdom.

> If asked to explain our methods, I would say: *firstly, we do not fish in other people's waters, or try to set up a rival sect.* Out of the gutters we pick our Converts, and if there be one man worse than another our Officers rejoice the most over the case of that man.[58]

Booth went on to repudiate any idea of the Army becoming "respectable." "'That is not our plan. We are moral scavengers, netting the very sewers. We want all we can get, but we want the lowest of the low.'"[59] The Army believed in a complete work of salvation amongst the most depraved.

> ... Can these poor creatures, captive, be delivered? Saved from sinning, saved into holy living, and triumphant dying? Saved now? The desponding answer will be "Impossible!" Ask multitudes of professing Christians and they will fear it is impossible. Ask the Salvationist, and the answer will be from both theory and experience, that the vilest and worst can be saved to the uttermost, for all things are possible to Him that believeth.[60]

The Army did not pursue the lowest of the low simply to fill up seats in some hall. It wanted them as soldiers and officers in the Army of Salvation. Railton said: "Best of all was the demonstration that, out of such material, God was able and ready to raise up a fighting force."[61] The question of salvation and ministry was, for the Army, a question about the power of God and not the depravity or weakness of man. God could save and use anyone. Booth declared:

> I care little about the size of the vessel; your intellect and learning and capacities may not be very extensive, but God will do wonders by you if your soul is only in sympathy with Him, and full of desperate determination to have souls or perish in the attempt.[62]

Mrs. Booth wrote:

> ... he requires us to break the bread of life to the multitude, trusting in Him for the supply. He hath *chosen* the weak things of the world to confound the mighty. Why? That the excellency of the power may be seen to be of God, and not of man.[63]

This conviction of the power of God, the significance of man in his sight, and the dynamic relationship between the two encouraged a concept of missions ahead of its time. In Booth's diary, a meeting in a small African village was described. It was attended by all classes of natives. Booth drew attention to an old woman Salvationist who had come from Somerset East with a big drum. Booth shook hands with her and gave her a copy of *Aggressive Christianity*.

Railton observed in this event that

> That union of races and languages to the glory of Christ, and for the highest well-being of the whole world; that valuing of the humblest true Soldier of the Cross above all the great ones of this world, accounts for the creation, maintenance and spread of the Army wherever they are seen.[64]

From the very beginning, the Army's goal was to raise up a native army under the leadership of its own people, and this was accomplished in many mission fields within a relatively short time.

The early Army believed literally in a God of all people; a God of men and women and boys and girls; a God of the high and the low. An American lady, prejudiced against the Army, attended one of its meetings. At first she was appalled by the form of worship, which she considered to be irreverence and sensationalism, especially so because it was the expression of ". . . 'raw-boned, coarse-faced men and women.'. . ."[65] But before the meeting was over she witnessed that "the Lord has taught me...through them already - that I can call *nothing* common or unclean."[66] In a society that was most sensitive to class distinctions, the Army obliterated those distinctions and saw only two classes that were really important, the saved and the unsaved. The Army committed itself to bringing about only one class, the saved.

The burden and obsession to save the world using *all* people was a radical interpretation of the Priesthood of the Believer. This was one of the lessons the Army believed it brought to the world.

> But one thing seems so abundantly clear in the history of our teaching and of its influence—so clear that I often marvel it is so little noticed by those who consider our Movement. I mean this—that the very spread of The Army does itself bear witness to the message we have proclaimed from the beginning—*that the Holy Spirit will come down on all the Lord's people if they seek Him.* The bishop, as my dear Father used to say, has no advantage in this over the washerwoman: the poor

Congo rubber-getter in his lash driven toil may be as favoured in this matter as the refined aristocrat who profits by his far off agony; the factory-girl is on equality here with the doctor of divinity.[67]

The idea of the priesthood of *all* believers was a concept consciously pursued by the Army in its formative years. The editor of *The Officer* wrote:

Some murmurs have reached us . . . as to whether "The Officer" may not defeat its good intentions and cut its own throat, so to speak, by converting *officers* into *preachers*. It is rumored that at some corps the soldiers and sergeants never have a chance, except in the open-air, the captain reserving all the indoor meetings to himself. Surely this is an exaggeration. The General is going to deal with this danger in a future number. Let us be awake to it, and do our utmost to avoid the snare.[68]

The Army found the established Church less than excited with the idea that the most common people also might be called to the ministry.

The whole religious world protested at this doctrine when we set it forth *in actual practise!* . . . It was said that we were *degrading* religion—that we brought Christianity into *contempt* by using these humble, uneducated, untrained agents to spread it . . . .[69]

One writer, known only by initials, printed an open letter to The General and his new Army, criticizing its position.

Doubtless at first you, and your immediate assistants, may have been helped forward by the *theoretical* writings of such men as Finney, who suppose, *or write as though they did so,* that the power of God is at the beck of every man, who can work a syllogism before Him on his knees with irreverent boldness, and then jump up, under the impulses of a faith of the fleshly mind, and take it for granted that he is called of God to act according to the verbal mission given to the disciples of old.[70]

A Catholic magazine criticized this idea as egotistical.

Egotism is of the very essence of the system. Each man and woman assumes to be a chosen vessel of the Holy Ghost, bound to look after the souls of others, and to lead them on by the aggressive manifestation of his or her own example. The advise of David, "Serve the Lord with fear, and rejoice unto Him with trembling," has no significance in their practise. They hold themselves to have that "perfect charity, (which) casteth out fear," of which St. John speaks.[71]

The Army found in this criticism an elitism which bred mediocrity within the Church. It believed that the Church's idea of God was too small and thus their perception of his salvation for all men was much underestimated. Booth warned his officers and soldiers that Scripture taught something quite different from the prevailing notion.

> . . . *cautioning all of us against what is narrow;* warning us against the snare which has thwarted God so much in His dealings with man in the past—*the snare of measuring what* HE *can do by what* WE *can do, and of measuring what we can do by the doings of the people round about us!*[72]

Booth argued:

> . . . we have been against the little ideas of little people as to what God could do for the world; yea, we have been altogether against *a little God!* We have even declared that a little God was almost as bad as no God.[73]

This attitude encouraged the idea of a personal God, and, for the Army, God was essentially "person" and not "being." "He" breathed into man the breath of life. There is no abstraction here whatsoever. Bramwell Booth said: ". . . in some of our efforts to approach Him we are perhaps in danger in this, that we do not as really, as consciously realise the fact that He is a person as we might."[74] Divine presence was intimately related to human life. God was so close to the members of the Army that when they spoke of Army mission it was synonymous with God's mission. However, this sense of divine incarnation was a radical departure from the popular position. Some of the Army's critics instead saw man replacing God.

> Is it only a few words that are wrong? Is not the whole spirit and tone, "we are the people"? It is not the responsibili-

ty of all Christians to "come to the help of the Lord against the mighty," to see to it that they are not slumbering and sleeping while the Lord is calling for labourers in His vineyard, but the *responsibility of all Christians towards* the *Salvation Army*.[75]

For many, the Army brought God too close. There was too much intimacy, too much familiarity. A catholic writer expressed his concern in this matter.

> ... it indulges in a familiarity with holy things that is some-times painful to Catholic ears. The Holy Name of Jesus is bandied about in songs which are profane, ribald, and almost blasphemous. It is shouted out in the "rollicking choruses" which General Booth speaks of with enthusiasm, in a way utterly at variance with the reverence due to the Name before which all in Heaven and on earth should bow. This ... in itself, proves that it cannot be regarded as a work of the Holy Spirit of God. For true religion not only includes a spirit of reverence, but it is in itself an act of reverence.[76]

Other critics saw in this radical intimacy a liability in the pursuit of Christian maturity. Pratt observed that in Army worship

> ... there seems little real and deepening repentance and growing faith in the Lord Jesus Christ; there seems no room for real spiritual devotion, no recognition of the Christian Sacraments, no culture of that truest Christian grace, humility.[77]

Pratt presented the popular view of religion, far more subdued and removed from God than the Army view he criticized.

> ... all this competing one with another ... as soon as it has ceased to excite curiosity or draw attention, as it soon will cease, will only make those who have suffered from it less dis-posed than ever towards that true repentance which scarce dare lift up its eyes to heaven, but smites upon its breast with a "God be merciful to me a sinner;" less disposed than ever for a religion that teaches us to seek above all the grace or true humility; for a religion that makes the test of its reality and sincerity the humble fulfillment of our daily duties; the daily prayer in secret for daily forgiveness; the daily cleansing of

our hearts from daily sins and infirmities; the faithful use of God's holy Sacraments and appointed means of grace; and the bringing forth of the fruit of the Spirit in ever deepening humility, and then the patient, cheerful fulfillment of our duty towards God and our duty towards our neighbour.[78]

Finally, this radical intimacy affirmed by the Army was regarded as an insult to the holiness and dignity of God.

Has the holy reverence that breathes in every word anything in common with the unseemly familiarity, with rushing into that presence with the assurance of equals, with the exuberance of animal spirits and excitement almost without bounds, with a light and easy use of sacred names suggested to most (to say the least), of levity and utter unseemliness, if we must not go farther and say even profanity?[79]

However, many of the disfranchised who had felt disowned for so long, found comfort, hope, and inspiration in the idea of a God who was not far off and not class conscious. That God could relate to them, even desire to dwell in their hearts, was a welcome relief from the coldness they perceived in Victorian, religious respectability. There were enough sovereigns, lords, and masters over them. They needed a friend somewhere, and the Army offered them Christ, a friend as well as Savior and Lord. Right or wrong, this radical intimacy with God was a heartthrob of the early Army. Bramwell Booth, in discussing prayer, wrote:

"It is not the point how long we spend, the point is whether we can come close up to Him and ask Him and feel ourselves, 'Yes, I speak to Him; He hears me; I know He is with me.'"[80]

Commissioner Frank Smith, discussing God as Father, wrote: "In these days a human lord is usually a very high-toned, difficult-to-get-at sort of affair—way up and out of reach of ordinary beings . . . ."[81]

"How considerate of Christ to reveal to man the Divine One in words so simple and yet so full of meaning.! For when these two words, 'Our Father,' are uttered, distance vanishes. . . ."[82]

The Army had a high view of man in his saved condition. It took quite literally his elevation to brotherhood with Christ. The angels veiled their faces before God, but the person who was born-again was raised higher than the angels and encouraged to come boldly before the throne of the Father in the spirit of joy and there to move and have his being. In salvation and sanctification, God and Man were to be truly reconciled, both in faith and works. Upon this understanding of God and man, the foundation of the Church might have been laid. Man's importance and possibilities in partnership with God, as well as his sense of belonging, could have been the foundation of a church. However, in the expression of these theological concepts, something other than a traditional understanding of the Church was laid upon this foundation. It became rather a movement with a peculiar understanding of itself as a religious body.

Part III

A Dramatic Theology

Chapter IX
Introduction

P art I presented a period of English history characterized by the Industrial Revolution and a social and
economic philosophy that exalted education and culture. These circumstances resulted in a climate of cool ratio-
nalism that disfranchised millions of Englishmen economi-
cally, socially, and spiritually.

The Salvation Army was born as part of a Church movement that included a wide theological spectrum of beliefs
and schemes. This movement tried to bring the disfranchised masses back into the Church and into a positive, har-
monious relationship with the rest of English society. The
Salvation Army began as one of many religious missions to
the poor and disfranchised masses. Its social assistance programs evolved from its spiritual concern over the eternal
welfare of immortal souls, who faced either eternal life or
eternal death, depending upon how they lived their lives on
earth. This theology was a direct expression of the evangelical theology of the eighteenth and nineteenth centuries. In
doctrinal formulation it was a direct derivative of
Methodism. In fervency and urgency it maintained the spirit of the Revival Movement of the nineteenth century.

Part II outlined the theological constructs or ideas that were foundational in the Army's spiritual and social concerns. In the emphases placed upon the doctrines of salvation and sanctification, the supernatural aspects of spiritual life were integrally related to the natural. Human problems were regarded as essentially spiritual in nature. The intimate and personal intervention of God in each individual life was considered by the Army to be absolutely necessary to meet acceptably and ultimately the need of salvation for both high and low, rich and poor, educated and uneducated. Salvation was considered to be foundational for proper behavior.

It would be misleading to suggest that the Army alone espoused these convictions and preached them with urgency. As noted, there was a spirit of revival in Victorian England. There was a new and powerful emphasis upon conscious, personal, individual relationships between God and man. However, The Salvation Army was the only new denomination to be established during this flurry of religious activity. Within a short time it had a significant number of members in many countries of the world. Why did it achieve a success so peculiar to its time? This is the concern of Part III.

There was more to the peculiar success of The Salvation Army than the doctrines it formulated. Theological constructs were not the only determinants in the establishment of The Salvation Army as a significant international social and religious institution. It was not the power of preaching alone, informing a spiritually ignorant public of poor, needy people that God loved them and wanted them as part of his family, that won converts to the Army.

The Army confronted a deeper cultural need among the masses than economic, social and religious disfranchisement. It confronted a cultural need, metaphysical in essence, a deprivation of the faith side of human nature, that aspect of human essence that engages in intuition, anticipation, hope, and trust. Here is the realm of the "resolve of will" where deep, daring, pervasive behavioral change is accomplished. This realm was not confronted by preaching alone; it was impacted by the dramatic way the Army expressed its theology.

It was the drama of theological expression that reached into a cold chamber of human personality and rekindled the sparks of faith and vision and put feet, arms, body, and heart around ordinary theological doctrines making them powerful ideas. It is in Part III that we come to grips with this concept of dramatic theological expression and the cultural circumstances that made it so important and effective.

.

Chapter X

A Metaphysical Problem in Victorian Culture

I t is not an overstatement to say that theologies and philosophies of history have moved the world toward self-understanding. Theology and philosophy alone have the capacity for discussing the essential concerns of knowing and being. Through these two conceptual exercises, mankind has tried to come to a knowledge of itself and that which is around and beyond it.

In nineteenth-century England, the theological and philosophical exercises grappling with the subject matter of "knowing" and "being" resulted in a peculiar cultural context. In a very real, though unconscious sense, two different cultural expressions were brought together. Two unique perceptions of reality confronted each other in tense conflict. One of these cultural expressions is characterized primarily by faith, emotion, and the infinitude of truth and reality. This study refers to this context as an image culture. In an image culture, essential truth and reality are seen through symbols and not directly. In this sense, truth and reality can never be fully grasped. They have an infinite quality about them that defies the limitations of the finite mind. The individual is caught up in an idea of truth and reality that is infinitely greater than he or she.

However, truth and reality are not to be thought of as plums dangling just beyond one's reach, always enticing but ever eluding one's grasp. Truth and reality form the very world of which the person is a part. Truth and reality are all around and a part of the person. They form a plot of land, the bounds of which can never be reached, but the grounds of which can be traversed and investigated to the heart's content. The more one travels through life, the closer one observes it, the better is one's discernment and the more one understands himself and defines his place in the world. This is culture in which the emotive character of a person is primary and where reason nurtures and develops that emotional character of human nature.

This cultural phenomenon is most apparent in the eras preceding the invention of the printing press, the proliferation of books, and the development of experimental science and statistical analysis. It is seen in medieval art where the representative figures are not analyzed to break down the picture into respective parts, but rather studied to build a picture of infinite perspective. To look at the art of the ceiling of the Sistine Chapel is to bring forth from the observer a response of awe that defies words and upon closer investigation completely exhausts them. The heart is left pounding, the mind racing in a hundred directions at once, not in an effort to capture and contain everything before its eyes, but to explore and be a part of it all.

This culture is identified in those ecclesiastical institutions of medieval times called monasteries and the monastic or disciplined life. The monastery was the seat of learning, one of the forerunners of the university, the place where knowledge was collected, sifted, recorded, and disseminated. Much more than this, it was a way of life. In fact, the monastic life was considered to be the best way of life reserved for only a select few. The monastery used education as a means to develop the devotional and social expression of community life. The disciplined life characterized by worship and contemplation was primary and these emphases answered the emotional needs of human nature firstly and the rational needs secondarily. The monk *felt* his place in God's economy and *felt* God's presence close to him. It was for that *feeling* that he came apart from the world. Later, universities developed primarily for those not wanting the monastic life but desiring to study nonetheless.

Consider the cathedrals. Their architecture appeals to man's emotive nature. To stand in the midst of a cathedral was to be immersed and dwarfed in the infinite magnitude of Almighty God. It was to be surrounded by a truth and reality of God that put his relationship with man into stark perspective, and made him feel his place in God's economy. The theology of the cathedral spoke to the worshipper through the panorama of sight that moved the emotions rather than in rational discourses of philosophical and theological constructs.

The old feudal society embodied an image culture. It was an ordered society where everyone had a place with privileges and obligations. The parts of society went together to make up the whole. Society was pulled together into one dominant expression of life characterized by order. People might be dreadfully poor, but they belonged, they had a place. Even the poorest had some semblance of emotional security.

With the invention of the printing press and the widespread dissemination of knowledge in written form, a change in culture took place. Walter Ong, in his book *The Presence of the Word*, argued that

> ... the development of writing and print ultimately fostered the break up of feudal societies and the rise of individualism. Writing and print created the isolated thinker, the man with the book, and downgraded the network of personal loyalties which all cultures favor as matrices of communication and as principles of social unity.[1]

The world moved from an image culture to a culture dominated by the "word." Somehow, written words seemed to have the capacity to capture truth, to analyze it and define it. Culture dominated by the printed word implied that anything that could not be put into print and explained was less real, less important, and less worthwhile. Ong criticized this implication:

> . . . a literate culture tends to overrate verbatim repetition or record. In literature cultures the illusion is widespread that if one has the exact words someone has uttered, one has by that very fact exact meaning. This is not true.[2]

Ong discussed this in terms of sound as opposed to the written word. Talking about sound, he said:

> Its reality eludes diagrammatic representation. This is a hard truth for technological man to accept: to him the measurements in space appear to be what is real and sound, but quite the opposite is true—the diagrams are unreal by comparison with sound as a psychological actuality.[3]

Could reality be so objectified as to make its meaning absolute? Ong said no, but Victorian England strongly implied yes.

The quest for knowledge became an occupation or exercise rather than a way of life. Analysis was a key concept and words were the vehicles for careful analysis and detailed explanation. The scholastic endeavor was to take the complex and to break it down into its simplest form. The vision of one immersed in an inexhaustible sea of reality, there to explore, search, study, and find one's being was replaced by the idea of man attacking the problems of truth and reality, in order to dominate them and put them to useful service.

A word culture argued that man could master reality, see it as it is, and in that mastery gain the answer to every problem of the human situation. The mystery of life was not so much something that awed a person and inspired a reverence for life because he was such a small and limited part of the whole; it was more a problem to be solved. Truth and reality were no longer sacred and approached in fear and trembling. Now, the person was sacred, with truth and reality the mud and clay to be discovered through intellect and molded by individual ingenuity. Symbols, such as art and architecture or the symbolical life of the monastery, were no longer lenses through which to view reality even though dark and blurred. Now symbols were forms to be analyzed, studied, and explained away in words that revealed reality in its naked, clear, concise "truth."

This kind of word culture dominated Victorian England, the England of The Salvation Army. W. Hastie, in his book *Theology As Science,* written in the nineteenth century, argued that

> Pre-scientific knowledge is mainly the work of the imagination still absorbed in sense, and it consists largely of the transference of mere subjective images or fancies to the objects of external perception which are thus invested with qualities and relations that do not really belong to them. This gives a certain poetic and mythical character to objects, which, on that stage of knowledge, are commonly personified and animated, and made in the image of the subject-mind thus apprehending them.[4]

Referring to scientific knowledge, Hastie went on to say:

> . . . knowledge becomes more and more objective, through the attempt, under a higher distinction to know things as they are in themselves. Its first step onward then consists in the rejection of mere inward ideas or fancies about objects, the purgation of knowledge from this unconscious subjective addition, and the establishment of an objective method under the sway of which knowledge now assumes a more perfect form and thereafter rapidly grows in content.[5]

As noted, the individual was preeminent. He broke through the symbols to naked truth and put truth into exact definition in words. Ong pointed out that

> ". . . oral cultures . . . hardly produce individual thinkers or inventors as do cultures where writing, and particularly the

alphabet, has become deeply interiorized and given the individual relative independence of the tribe."[6]

This exaltation of the individual rested on a high view of man which encouraged little sympathy for the social "failure," as the poor were considered to be.

However, the poor were not the only group of people who experienced a problem in this culture dominated by the word. There was another segment of society, oddly enough at the other end of the social scale, that felt alienated. They were the intellectuals. However, what was impossible for the poor to do, the intellectuals accomplished. They discovered the cause of disfranchisement. They recognized that the popular world view depreciated the emotive aspect of human nature.

A utilitarian society seemed to have captured the mystery of life in the discovery of the mechanical nature of the universe. The intellectuals saw this mechanical view as partial and destructive. Carlyle in his *Signs of the Times* pointed out that "the domain of mechanism . . . can at any time embrace but a limited portion of man's interests, and by no means the highest portion."[7] Man's dynamic, emotional nature was sadly overlooked in the mechanical view, and only this dynamic, emotional aspect of man could delve into ". . . the mysterious springs of Love, and Fear, and Wonder, of Enthusiasm, Poetry, Religion, all which have a truly vital and *infinite* character. . . ."[8]

> This faith in Mechanism, in the all-importance of physical things, is in every age the common refuge of Weakness and blind Discontent; of all who believe, as many will ever do, that man's true good lies without him, not within.[9]

In *Sartor Resartus* Carlyle criticized the mechanism of utilitarianism for making him miserable. He was miserable because he was always thinking of his self-interest, his pleasure. This was a sad second to the higher motives of Virtue, Faith, and

Hope. The universe as a machine is impersonal, dead, a "steam engine" dominating man and crushing the life out of him. Carlyle argued that in reality the universe is essentially spiritual. The material world must be understood as only a symbol of the spiritual, whose essence is found not through reason alone, but by intuition, feeling. Carlyle concluded that no one has a *right* to be happy, so man is not to pursue pleasure. He called people back from the empiricism, materialism, and mechanism of middle-class philosophy, once more to pursue God, and God was to be found in a reverence for nature where the infinite blends with the finite.

Tennyson, like Carlyle, emphasized the spiritual side of nature in his poem *In Memoriam*. The science of his day had revealed a hard, impersonal, comfortless picture of nature, which called into question immortality, progress, and an existant divine plan. In spite of all this, Tennyson affirmed the existence of a spiritual reality, not on any rational basis but rather on an intuitive basis of faith. Faith alone can understand the spiritual. To apply reason alone to the consideration of nature limits the contribution of nature to the understanding of life. Tennyson exposed the doubt that the mechanical view brought to nineteenth-century Englishmen and resolved that doubt by positively affirming and exalting faith over reason.

J. S. Mill, perhaps the greatest spokesman for utilitarianism and yet one of the chief critics of Benthamite Utilitarianism, had his doubts about this view of reality that summed up ethics in the happiness principle and exalted the individual. Along with Benjamin Disraeli's conclusions in *Sybil*, Mill recognized that to view man as being motivated by pleasure alone was too simplistic. Man's character was relational or social, and Mill and Disraeli asserted that happiness could not be a direct goal. Man must seek the good of others, not his own self-interest. Self-interest is inadequate, a direct attack on Benthamite Utilitarianism and individualistic, mechanistic, middle- class thought. Against this mechanical view, which said that through man's search for happiness the good would automatically prevail, Mill asserted that the good (happiness) comes when man feels right.[10]

Happiness is generated from within a person and not from outside, and the intellectuals all agreed that reason alone was inadequate for an accurate perception of reality. A place for the imaginative, intuitional, emotional side of man was necessary for wholeness.

Carlyle argued that this mechanical world view, dominated by a natural law of cause and effect, produced a tragic dilemma for the poor. In *Past and Present* he asserted that death was not what made man wretched. What made man wretched was ". . . to live miserably we know not why; to work sore and yet gain nothing; . . . to die slowly all our life long, imprisoned in the deaf, dead, Infinite Injustice. . . ."[11]

Both the intellectuals and the poor were imprisoned in a world view which was too narrow for them. The intellectuals lived in a philosophical and social climate where all of the parameters of truth, right, and good seemed to have been uncovered. This left very little room for the expression of imagination and creativity which were preeminent concerns for this select group of people. They and that which was most dear to them were put in the background for something more "useful," more practical, the tangibles of life like wealth and power. The intellectuals fought this restructuring of reality in their writing and this in itself gave them hope.

It was another story for the poor. They did not think in terms of the restructuring of reality. They were faced with survival itself. Their lives hung on the thread of abject poverty and were threatened with extinction by a way of life that seemed to have all the answers and regarded poverty as an ill with its roots in the individual and not in the very concepts of reality that reigned. The restructuring of reality that took place in the development of a dominating word culture not only left the poor without a home in their land, but also without a hope in their hearts.

Victorian social pressure demanded that the masses put their houses in order. They were belittled for their lack of self-discipline and criticized for their earthiness. They found nothing but distain for their shortcomings. For their critics, the answer to their problem was a matter of commonsense reasoning that "anyone" could understand. However, predominantly illiterate and unqualified, they were unprepared to understand their situation, let alone argue their case. Unable to oppose the rationale of Utilitarian philosophy, in frustration and hostility they rebelled against social and religious pressure. The problem was not as simple as society thought. It was not essentially a problem of lack of character or talent or sincere effort but of culture. The masses lived with a different cultural reference which was outdated and depreciated by the ruling philosophy.

The impoverished masses of Victorian England—perhaps 75% of the population—were the remaining remnants of an image-oriented culture. One of McLeod's observations of the masses, cited in Chapter IV, implied an image-culture characteristic. The masses of London tended to withdraw into a more local world, their own neighborhood. Whether or not it was considered to be modern tribalism or older feudalism, it was a cultural referent of a past day encouraged by a sense of threat and anxiety. The poor needed each other. Another of McLeod's observations of the masses was that the better-paid workers who sought out a church home sought one where the blood of Christ was more prominent than the Sermon on the Mount, and where abstinence from drink, oaths, and tobacco were important symbols of their faith. As in image cultures, where symbols were used to engage the mysterious, emphasizing the emotional dimension of life, the masses still lived at the emotional and mysterious edge of reality. The lives of the poor who labored from night to night and had nothing, and the millions who did not have even a job at which to labor, were filled with questions that seemed to have no answers. These lives were filled with anguish, anxiety, anger, fear, shame, and hopelessness. They could appreciate emotion and drama far more than rational argument or doctrinal discourse. However, there was little place for that emotion which formed the very core of their being.

Before the Army came into being, there was already a technical term used to describe appeals directed to the emotional side of man. It was "sensationalism." In Victorian England, it was opposed most forcefully. One of the religious movements criticized for sensationalism was Primitive Methodism. Bairstow wrote of their religious expression in the early camp meetings. "The people were drawn together by sights and sounds which aroused their attention and curiosity, and then they were fed by the kind of food they could digest."[12] In 1879, still criticized as sensationalistic, *The Primitive Methodist Quarterly Review* confronted the issue and attempted to define "Sensationalism." According to the writer,

> . . . the production of a sensation is not, in itself, an evil thing in eloquence, and cannot be regarded as that which we designate sensationalism. The mischief lies in the prominence given to the sensation as an end in and of itself, and in the nature of the sensation as being out of harmony with the great purpose which every preacher of the gospel ought to have in view, and with the associations of the place in which his discourse is given.[13]

Sensationalism was considered to result from a wrong motive.

> Instead of seeking to "present every man perfect in Christ Jesus," he desires instant appreciation of his own performance. He sets a trap for the applause of his audience, and

when that comes he has his reward. He does not seek to persuade, but to please, or to exhilarate, or to startle, or to excite, and so descends from the lofty position of the sacred orator to the lower level of the actor. He is not forbidden to do any of these things provided they be not in themselves irreverent or rediculous, and provided, also, they be made by him conducive to the highest interest of his hearers.[14]

Sensational titles for sermons or announcements of meetings were opposed because they made ". . . the gathering of a large assemblage the primary object of the preacher; while the spiritual instruction of the people is treated as secondary and subordinate."[15] In conclusion it was argued that sensationalism depraved taste and blunted sensibilities so that hearers were not moved by ordinary presentations of truth. As a result, exhilaration was sometimes mistaken for Christian experience.[16] The problem was that the parameters of sensationalism as defined could only be subjectively adjudicated. There were no real objective criteria. In the rationalistic context of Victorian England, sensationalism seemed to be applied to anything that expressly touched the emotions.

The term sensationalism was applied to The Salvation Army very easily and often with a vengeance. An author, known only by his initials, argued that sensationalism not in accord with the mind of God was characterized in the Army by young women who grabbed hold of the Army flag and vowed to stay devoted to its principles until death.[17] The red of the Army flag stands for salvation through the blood of Jesus, the yellow for the purging and power of the Holy Spirit in the Christian life, and the blue for the purity of holiness which should characterize every Christian. These are principles to which many students of the ministry might be expected to commit themselves even in Victorian England in 1882. It is not clear whether grabbing the flag was sensational or the fact that a woman did it. The same author asserts that "Appeals to the senses have ever characterised corrupt forms of worship."[18]

In the early years, the Army's methods made it anathema for churchgoer and nonchurchgoer alike. The barroom brawlers saw the Army people as holier-than-thou do-gooders poking their noses into places they did not belong. A band of ruffians called themselves the Skeleton Army and literally waged war against Booth's soldiers trying to drive them from the streets, the neighborhoods, and existence itself.

The leading article of *The Times*, June 14, 1882, supported the Army's right to march, even though it was a repulsive movement.

> The Salvation Army may be neither very judicious nor very conciliatory in its operations. The assumption of the title "Army" with all its grades and ranks, the copious use of military metaphors in describing the objects of its campaign, its independence, and its pugnacious activity are all calculated to provoke opposition and antagonism. But, notwithstanding this, so long as it abides by the law, it is clearly entitled to the protection of the law.[19]

The professional clergy despised the vulgar pounding of the drum, the dissonant brass bands, the loud Amens and Hallelujahs. A Catholic magazine charged that Salvation Army religion was ". . . not so much the religion of the poor as the religion of the vulgar. Its phraseology, its hymns, its addresses, its newspapers, continually offend against good taste."[20] Another writer asserted that this expressive worship lacked any "notion of reverence."[21] Attacking the Army's use of familiar and sensational language regarding God and the supposed work of the Holy Spirit in the Army, a writer argued:

> Of course I shall be met with the old argument urged in favour of all revival movements, "O, but look at the *fruits*, see how God 'honours' these people and 'owns' their labour of love"! I contend that in examining their literature—the language which they deliberately commit to writing and offer for sale as samples—I *am* "looking at fruits," of a *much* more convincing and less doubtful character than any lists of prisoners

sent to headquarters. . . .[22]

In a commentary on Army posters which gave graphic description to the spiritual war and presented all the meeting activities in war-like terms, a shocked critic wrote:

> No one who has any reverence for divine things can read this placcard without being filled with a sense of shame, horror, and disgust. Well might Lord Shaftesbury, in referring to it at a meeting on Saturday, remark that "the excesses of the Army were producing great irreverence of thought, of expression, and of action, turning religion into a play, and making it grotesque."[23]

Discussing the possibility of uniting The Salvation Army with the Church of England, one writer declared that,

> No amount of good effected (as they assert) by the Salvationists can justify the use of profane and even blasphemous language so closely connected with it, united to a style of action more suited to the pantomime of a theatre than the solemn worship of Almighty God. They are undoubtedly breaking the Third Commandment, and bringing our holy religion into contempt. Religion though a joyful is a very serious thing, and quite incompatible with irreverence and grotesque performances. May we, therefore, hope that the attempt to unite the "Army" with the church of England may never be carried out without a total change in their language and present mode of worship.[24]

John Price, purporting to test the Army by its works, wrote:

> . . . let me call the knowing ones, the leaders and editors, the actors and actresses in this hateful caricature of all that is sacred and holy, to a repentance which they need *far* more than the ignorant "masses" whom they compare to "the inhabitants of Sodom and Gomorrah!"[25]

When sensationalism was charged it was the appeal to emotion or feeling that was being critized. Feeling in religion was seriously suspect. *The Church Quarterly Review* expressed a distrust of Booth's darkest England scheme because it sprang

... from the stress laid upon what must generally be a mere change of feeling, which is spoken of as "finding salvation," or "being saved," and from the complete ignoring of the sacraments. The immense importance attached to the former of these, is thus described in the *Doctrine of The Salvation Army*, a book purporting to be written by "General" Booth: *'Never tell them that they are saved if they don't think so.* When a man gets saved God will tell him about it, and then he will not need you to tell him so.'[26]

In *The Month*, the Army's mystical sense of salvation is criticized as resting on the sandy foundation of feeling.

... the religion of the Salvation Army ... certainly requires no internal obedience of heart and will. In order to "find Christ," to be "converted," to be "saved," there is no need of humility. There are no dogmas to be accepted. Salvationism is a religion without a theology, without ritual, and without sacraments, and such a religion cannot last. It has no backbone. It is a matter of feeling and of sentiment. There is no subjection of the intellect. Hence it is not only compatible with pride and self-will, but rather provokes them by the conviction it implants that he who accepts it is "saved," and therefore a superior being to those around him who have not passed through the mystic process.[27]

The daughter of a Mr. Samuel Charlesworth accompanied Booth's daughter Eva to Switzerland and there received notoriety in *The Times* when she was brought to trial in Switzerland for certain activities of The Salvation Army. Her father recalled that ". . . the Salvation Army took a strong hold upon her imagination, and she became fascinated with its meetings and work."[28] The father attended some Army meetings with his daughter and reported:

I shrank with trembling from the responsibility of allowing a child of so sensitive a nature and impulsive a disposition to be subject to the intense excitement called forth in those meetings, the whole work being so essentially based and carried on by exciting appeals to the feelings. But I found with sorrow that my daughter had been already so wrought upon by the system that no other form of worship satisfied her spiritual cravings.[29]

The early Army was aware of this conscious prejudice against emotion. Mrs. Booth, whose ministry did reach out to the middle and upper classes, recognized this bias in one of her letters to her son Bramwell.

> I worked for fifteen of the best years of my life exclusively amongst the middle and upper class people . . . , and I always found that until they yielded to the Spirit of God in their own souls, any expression of *feeling*, however modest, was distasteful to them.[30]

In a culture dominated by the word, society was looking for comfort in a sense of factual certainty. If one went according to a prescribed formula or set of instructions, one could assume that things would work out properly. One need not worry about feeling which could be terribly misleading. Applied to the theology of salvation it resulted in a sort of instrumental approach accomplished through proper understanding and obedience to religious principles of respectability. However, in the nineteenth century, this view began to concern some members of the religious community. *The Primitive Methodist Quarterly Review* raised the question between sensationalism and heartless intellectualism. Dr. William M. Taylor wrote:

> . . . much as we dislike sensationalism, and greatly as we deplore the evils to which it leads, we are far from believing that it is the only or the chief danger of the pulpit in these days. We have more fear, on the one hand, of that heartless intellectualism which, by its uniform appeals to the head, develops a cold moderatism that leads at length to a positive unbelief; and, on the other hand, of that tepid sentamentalism which, in its method of proclaiming that "God is love," wipes out all moral distinctions and drugs conscience into sleep.[31]

A reserved, rationalistic intellectualism within religion was starving the spirits of people who lived by feeling. *The Christian Commonwealth* recognized this problem as the reason the people at the lower end of the social scale were not reached with Christianity.

> Mr. White denounced the teaching in some hymnals used, as not tending to raise the mind to a genuine emotion towards God. It appeared to him that the most grievous defect in their popular religious instruction for many years had been the abstract form of teaching and its unreal tone of feeling; and the result had been that Christianity had never reached, in a living form, the vast multitude of our lower people, who, although they had been to Sunday-school, had been abandoned to a power of evil unparalleled in [the] history of the world.[32]

In a book entitled *Christianity and the Working Classes*, edited by George Haw, one author described the Church of Victorian England as patronizing and stiff. "This stiffness goes with, and accounts for, that self-repression and objection to showing emotion, which has been the cause of many of our blunders at home and abroad."[33] ". . . there is no inconvenient expansion, and we try no new thing."[34]

> It cannot adapt itself; it would like to catch the ear and heart of all, but it is clumsy, and out of its element and therefore fails. The workers want to be moved and excited. In our people there is a deep well of wholesome emotion.[35]

Another writer, criticizing his own church, wrote: "Most of our efforts have in them neither, the deep, mysterious appeals of one side or the emotional stirring of the other side; we offer neither Roman mysteries nor the soul-swaying eloquence of the Salvationists."[36] At the turn of the nineteenth century, one writer lamented:

> The great symbols of faith are for the moment out of date. The brazen serpent is recognised to be a piece of brass. The Bible, the Church, the Sunday, the Creeds, the Services are seen to be other than they seemed. Symbols being in their nature dead, and thought being in its nature living, the symbols must from time to time be readapted to cover the new growth. These great symbols have not now the same relation to modern knowledge as they had to the knowledge of past generations. They are no longer, therefore, the powerful aids by which men's souls are brought into contact with the high-

est they know.[37]

When great symbols of faith are explained away, the depreciation of the feeling side of man and his religion also occurs. One writer referred to this faith side as the human side of man. He suggested that "it is from the lack of the humane side, a side as prominent in the Bible as that of any doctrine, that we owe much of the alienation of the working man."[38]

The theological constructs of the Army implied a sense of belonging for the alienated and dispossessed. But what was it that pursuaded the dispossessed to believe in, to hope for, to live and die for that home which though begun in this life transcended the ages of time? Something reached down to the very essence of human nature, the "resolve of will," which brought new faith and new vision to the disfranchised. Something met the cultural need of the deprivation of feeling and faith within the emotive nature of the hopeless.

Chapter XI

A Dramatic Expression of Theology in Literature

The Salvation Army brought into the religious circles of Victorian England an expression of theology that directly confronted the emotive nature of man. It was expressed in images and ideas that were powerful and peculiarly appropriate for the poorer classes caught up in a word culture that left them emotionally destitute, especially in the area of religion. This was a theology dramatically expressed.

Nowhere is the dramatic expression of the Army more clearly illustrated than in its own literature where the dramatic was not just implied but at times explicitly promoted. The introductory remarks of the Company Orders of 1909 (a Sunday school teachers' manual) contain a short play that was written to show how to study the Company Lesson (Sunday school lesson) at home. It was meant to be acted out at a Company Guard Meeting (Sunday school teachers' meeting) to help the Guards (Sunday school teachers) in their studies so that they could better present the lessons to the Juniors in their companies (classes). The play was titled "A Dialogue, Showing How to Study the Company Lesson at Home," and emphasized teaching through illustration and storytelling.[1] This teaching focused on the senses in an effort to *show* concepts to those who did not appreciate philosophical and theological discourse.

> The imagination of children is very vivid; they "see" what is well and clearly told. To so describe a Bible Story that it becomes living and actual is an art worth much patience and toil to gain. Every help towards description must be used, pictures, object actions, anything to bring the Lesson within their "ken."[2]

However, dramatic instruction was not relegated only to children. In the Army's earliest days as the *East London Christian Mission*, the mission's magazine encouraged aspiring ministers to approach the ministry through the eyes and the ears in order to strengthen their resolve to minister. The written expression is highly dramatic in its exhortation. The ministerial aspirants could *see* what they were being exhorted to do.

> Go through the town you live in, and take a clear survey of the wicked, and notice their sins. Count the flaming gin-palaces, beer-houses, tea-gardens, saloons, dancing-rooms, brew-houses, wine-vaults, brothels, play-houses, and other devil's chapels. Look at their desolation until your heart aches with grief on account of their damning sins. See the daring Sabbath-breakers with their open shops, brasen fronts, and hardened hearts. See the moving mass of prostitutes and their vile supporters, the seducers and the seduced, rushing madly together into everlasting burnings. Go through the filthy streets, dirty lanes, and dark squares, and try to find out the reigning sins of every family, if possible.[3]

Dramatic language is further illustrated in comparing two ways of saying substantially the same thing. The first statement on lay involvement in evangelism is typical of a more intellectual expression with little, if any, dramatic appeal.

> What our famed Liverpool Minutes say of every Methodist Minister is applicable to every Christian: he is bound to be in spirit "a Home Missionary," eagerly doing all he can to bring his kinsfolk and neighbors to Christ.[4]

This second statement is from *The Officer* magazine and is highly dramatic in nature.

> Upon the rocks of sin the immense ship "Humanity" has struck. Millions upon millions of doomed souls move about its decks and shriek for help. We cannot save them without risk, without suffering; it may be in saving them we may lose our own lives. Shall we hold back or press forward? Face the raging seas of opposition and rescue thousands![5]

Salvation Army literature is filled with this highly dramatic expression.

Another characteristic of this dramatic expression was the use of metaphor to illustrate spiritual truths. One of the message outlines in *The Officer* dealt with the gospel ship or the S.S. Salvation. The sermon content treated the *sea*—of time; the *vessel*—of salvation; *port bound for*—heaven; *time of departure*—now; *captain*—God himself; *cost of passage*—Christ's death; *passengers*—the saved; *chart*—the Bible; *rocks*—to be avoided; *storms*—to trust to God.[6] Of this literature, Inglis wrote: "Their use of topical secular images was typical of Army propaganda and preaching."[7] The book *Salvation Mine* takes the secular image of the mine and adapts it to the message of the Gospel. You do not need to read carefully to *hear* the sounds of soul anguish or to *see* the rescue teams going down into the abyss in search of lost miners.

> "WANTED, SALVATION MINERS!"
>
> Is the cry of Adam's bleeding heart. "Wanted, Salvation Miners!" is the advertisement of the skies. Set all telegraphs in motion. Lightenings, flash it! Thunders, peel it! Winds blow it! Angels carry it! Let all creation advertise: "Wanted, Salvation Miners!" Who will venture? Who will volunteer? Amid the stench and darkness, amid the gloom, and doom, and death, who will face the monster—put his foot on the Serpent's head, bear the wrath of an angry God, undertake to redeem and rescue a fallen world?[8]

In *The Officer*, 1894, there was an article concerning the importance of evangelism. It reported a dream or vision the editor of the magazine had regarding his own funeral. He used the article to express three regrets he had at his funeral. First, he regretted he had not spent more time with God; second, that he had not made more of his opportunities to search the heights and depths of the grace, power, revelation, and wisdom of God; and third, that he had not spent his time more powerfully compelling men to seek God. However, it is the dramatic nature of the written word that interests us.

> Why had I not poured more of the blood and fire of Heaven into each life and number? Why had not the burning realities of sin and death and hell been more dearly cast on every sheet? Why had not the trumpet-blasts of salvation of holiness been rung in louder notes throughout the world?[9]

The written material of The Salvation Army accurately represented its verbal proclamation; the Army wrote what it said. These written and verbal messages explained the practical expression of the Army. This relationship between written and verbal messages was significantly different from those of other religious and secular movements, which recognized a value in the emotional side of human nature.

The Settlement Movement had an appreciation for emotion and feeling. In Picht's report of the movement, he uncovered one of its assumptions. "A man who all day long sees nothing but work-rooms and desolate rows of houses, hears nothing but the rattle of machinery, has a craving for music and gay pictures."[10] The Settlement Movement hypothesized an aesthetical deprivation of the masses. It is illustrated further by a description given of Toynbee Hall.

> The Toynbee building is arranged as far as possible to suggest an English college. Entering a narrow arch from one of the noisiest streets, and passing through to the rear of a large warehouse, you find yourself in a covert, or "quad," so dear always to the heart of a university man. The windows, roof, and towers strengthen the impression. Vines grow on the walls, and there are window-boxes full of flowers. During the

day only a distant rumble is heard from the streets. In the evening the place is delightfully quiet. The good taste shown in the interior arrangements, especially the generous plan of the drawing-room and dining-room, completes the effect of making everything in harmony with the spirit of the undertaking. These surroundings serve to keep fresh the reminiscences of the residents, and, on the other hand, to bring the working people into something of the classic university atmosphere.[11]

For the university public there was an atmosphere conducive to the pursuit of knowledge and culture. The cultural pursuit and the surroundings supplemented each other and brought about a beauty that the university public mistakenly thought could and should be recognized by all people and especially the poor. Some churches found this beauty in appropriate liturgy where the message was combined with appropriate forms of worship. This resulted in an aestheticism of form. The Oxford Movement, which endeavored to bring some of the mystery and pomp of Roman Catholicism into Protestant circles, is an example of this emphasis. But not everyone had the same appreciation for religious aesthetics. Charles Waller recognized this in a sermon he preached in St. Paul's Church in 1882 on The Salvation Army and how Christians ought to judge the movement. In that sermon he felt constrained to deal with emotion and reason as both being appropriate to religion.

> Remember that we are creatures susceptible of feeling as well as capable of reasoning, and that it is through both of these avenues of the soul that religion comes to us. Within the Church of Christ, what is the effect wrought upon those who love to enter into a house of God which has been beautified by the art of man, rich in ceremonial and adornment? Do not these surroundings move such spirits to reverence, and predispose to worship? And if so are not their feelings worked upon before the spirit begins to articulate its worship? Or if it be the case that the house of God is simple in its neatness and unadorned, and the service as free from ritual ceremonial as possible, is it not true that the preacher well understands the composite nature of his hearers—that they have feelings as

well as intellect—and the style therefore of his preaching becomes emotional, stirring the feelings as well as endeavouring to reach the understanding?[12]

Waller makes a subtle comparison of two aspects within religion. He refers to art, ceremony, and adornment as aesthetics expressed in form. Later he refers to preachings that become emotional. This is a theology dramatic in nature.

Aesthetics did not go deep enough to meet the need of the disfranchised even though it touched the emotional side of a person. It was drama rather than aesthetics that met with significant success among the masses. In dramatic expression the message is not supplemented with expression as much as it is one with expression. The message is clothed with actors and images which very literally define that message. Word and image come together without losing their identities. This happened in much of the preaching and writing of the early Army. Every seminary student is taught the importance of illustrations to strengthen and clarify main points. But for the early salvationists, sermons and articles were filled with illustrations, and often, the whole sermon or article was an illustration.

The literature central to the Army's message, both written and preached, was the Bible itself. The Army was passionate in its conviction regarding the Bible, declaring it to be ". . . the only authorized and trustworthy written revelation of the mind of God. In this it stands alone not one among other such scriptures."[13] The same writer stated again:

> The Salvation Army claims for the Bible that it contains a revelation of the feelings of God toward us and of His wishes as to our conduct toward Him and our fellow men. It gives us everything in the way of a written revelation that is necessary to salvation, holy living and our welfare.[14]

Regarding the credibility of the Bible, the doctrine book of 1881 asserted:

> The Holy Spirit not only preserved these holy men from

mistake, and enabled them to write the *exact truth* concerning the facts they record, but also enabled them to *communicate* the *mind* and *will* of God to us.[15]

The Army tried to bring the biblical text to life for its youth so that they might know it and practice its truths. "Your duty in the Company meetings is to teach your children the Bible. True; but your duty is also so to teach them that the Bible will become to each of them a living power in their lives."[16]

> In these days, when there are so many false and misleading lights on every hand, it is of the greatest value for our Juniors to learn early where the only true light is to be found, and also the way in which to apply that light to their own hearts.[17]

This author asserted that the Juniors must be taught *"To feed themselves from the Bible . . . to find the right way through the light of the Bible. . . ."*[18] The Bible was not to be watered down in its presentation to children. The Company Orders for 1907 warned: ". . . beware of blunting its edges and dulling its point because 'it seems too dreadful to speak to children of Hell, or to read the curses of the Bible.'"[19] "There is a great deal of mock-mercy abroad in the world today. May the Sword of the Spirit in your hands be quick and powerful, sharp and piercing, and your work be first pure, then peaceable!"[20]

In the training of cadets, the Bible was equally preeminent. In a sketch of life at the International Training College this strong statement was found.

> Greatest stress is laid on the necessity, the absolute essential, of knowing the Bible, its characters, its history, its laws, its promises, and its threatenings. There are carefully condensed, simple, thorough lectures on the Bible every day, and Bible readings and study in private and public. A Cadet *may* fail in an examination on the "Doctrines." He or she *must not* fail in the examination on the Bible.[21]

The early Army preached the authority of Scripture to all people and institutions. Mrs. Booth lamented:

. . . I am afraid, that any practical quotation of the Bible in either of the Houses of our Legislature would only provoke laughter; that the suggestion of the alteration or stoppage of any measure because the Bible says this or that, would only provoke ridicule and scorn.[22]

She went on to encourage Salvationists:

Fix the anchor of your soul in these glorious proclamations of the Divine will, in these glorious prophetic announcements with which the Book abounds. Plod on patiently, work and struggle; weep and pray on. It will help to hasten this glorious consummation.[23]

Bramwell Booth, as general, wrote that ". . . the older I get, the more I see the precious influence and value of that glorious Message we call the Word of God. Oh, do stick to your Bibles, you Salvationists."[24]

The question is, in what sense did the Army consider Scripture a unique writing of God? When the Army spoke of the biblical message, what did it mean? These questions are important because their answers support the argument that the Army's perception of Scripture influenced its peculiar expression of theology.

The cornerstone of Salvation Army theology was a literal sense of Scripture. Thomas Aquinas is a most able resource in helping to explain what is meant by the term "literal sense of Scripture." Literal sense did not mean a literalism so chained to the definition of words as to disallow an interpretation of those word-meanings within the context in which they are found. Aquinas's discussion of God and body illustrates and is used to argue against an extreme literalism. His first point contained five arguments and presented the case that God did have a body. These arguments exhibited this extreme literalism in dealing with Scripture: (1) Anything that has dimensions has a body. Job 11:8-9 indicates God is higher than heaven, deeper than hell, longer than earth, and broader than the sea. Also, (2) bodies have shape and Genesis 1:26 reveals that man is made in the image and likeness of God. Image means figure and shape so God is body. Further, (3) parts of the body are ascribed to God: Job 40:4 talks about the arm of God; Psalms 117:6, the right hand of the Lord; Psalms 33:18, the eyes of the Lord. A body has posture and (4) God assumes postures: Isaiah 6:1—God sits; Isaiah 3:13—God stands. Lastly, (5) anything serving as a starting point or finishing point has to be a body. Scripture referred to God as both a starting point and a finishing point.[25]

To read the above passages literally was, according to Aquinas, to push the literal meaning to an inaccurate conclusion. How he argued against the above is not important here. What is important is his recognition that the literal sense of Scripture did not rule out metaphoric meanings. This understanding of metaphor was necessary if Scripture was to be interpreted so as to avoid self-contradiction. For example, to argue that God is a body because in Scripture eyes, arms, and postures are attributed to him, is to encounter difficulty when Scripture also clearly asserts that God is a spirit (John 4:24). That the literal sense must be understood to contain at least the possibility of a metaphorical sense if certain passages are to harmonize, is a rational, sensible approach to the hermeneutic problem.

Aquinas went on to argue that any spiritual senses of Scripture must be based on the literal sense of Scripture if confusion and contradiction were to be avoided.[26] Without this connection between the spiritual and the literal sense, confusion would reign.[27] Further, he argued that everything necessary for the faith was revealed openly through the literal sense of some passage of scripture. Van Der Ploeg translated Quod. VII as follows: ". . . Quodibetum (VII, art 15, ad 3) it is said: 'Nothing is taught mysteriously (Occulte) in any place of Scripture which is not explained clearly elsewhere . . . .'"[28] Thomas Aquinas was saying in the strongest terms that the literal sense alone was necessary for an understanding of the things of faith. In fact, no arguments could be drawn from the spiritual sense, only from the literal sense.

> Cogent arguments cannot be developed from the spiritual sense, not from any lack of authority, but because the symbolic interpretation of history is tricky business. One event may be figurative of so many others; if you start chopping and changing without taking care you may easily find yourself with a fallacious conclusion.[29]

In arguing against the Manichaean position on the incarnation, which asserted that Christ assumed an imaginary body, Aquinas pointed out that they were robbing the Scriptures of their authority. Scriptural authority rested in the literal reading of those passages that ascribed flesh, walking, eating, dying, being buried, to Jesus. These human, physical aspects were not to be interpreted symbolically because it was clear that the author *intended* to present Jesus as a *real* man. Thomas Aquinas argued that a whole incident like the life and death of Christ, cannot be related with a double meaning unless somewhere in the Scriptures the literal sense reveals the true meaning of the event. But, all the passages of Scripture referring to Christ, referred to him as a real man and nowhere was the contention supported that he was only an apparition. Aquinas asserted that when metaphor was used, the fact that it was metaphor was either clearly evident from the context or "stated elsewhere in Scripture in proper terms, which express the truth clearly."[30]

For Thomas Aquinas the literal sense was primary and definitive. It was the highest sense of Scripture. It alone could and must corroborate or validate a spiritual or symbolic meaning in some passage of Scripture. When the term "literal sense of Scripture" is used in this study, it is used in the Thomistic sense, as outlined above. This does not mean that the application of the above will always bring everyone to the same theological understanding. But it does mean that the early Army started from a point much akin to Aquinas. The literal sense was authoritative for them. If the literal sense appeared metaphorically, it was accepted as such. But it was the faith in the historicity of the Scriptures as well as the revelation of truth, which Scripture was believed to be, that formed the basis of Army theology and guided its hermeneutics. It was also this primacy of the literal sense of Scripture that provided an appropriate foundation for a dramatic expression of theology. Theologians like Bultmann and Tillich regarded this dramatic expression as myth or legend. They have endeavored in a sense to get beyond the literal sense to a meaning that speaks to the present generation. This has resulted in an abstraction that is difficult to express in mental images. It is reasoned, but it cannot be "seen" and for some it cannot be "felt." The debate over the view of Scripture and its interpretation was going on in Victorian England.

Kathleen Hessman, in her study of the work of Evangelicals in the Victorian Period, asserted:

> ... they were all agreed upon salvation by faith and the infallability and over-riding importance of the Scriptures. They all feared the growing influence of Roman Catholicism and the rapid spread of Tractarianism. They were united in their stand against rationalism and the theories of evolution which seemed to undermine the literal truth of the Bible. Even the works of a staunch Evangelical, such as Henry Drummond who tried to reconcile these new views with Evangelical theology, were regarded as suspect by many.[31]

In its formative years, the Army was surely in the company of the above; however, it was not actively engaged in the theological debate to any significant degree.

The Army accepted the literal sense of Scripture and attempted to harmonize it with everyday observations and circumstances. In the Company Orders for 1906, there was a note on the January 7 lesson lest students be puzzled by Elkanah's action. He was a holy man with two wives and was possessed of an apparent lack of regard for human life, willingly slaughtering enemies when this seemed to be the only way of dealing with them. The writer explained the concept of progressive revelation for the students.

> ... it is with the spiritual as it is with the natural light, the dawn comes to the earth gradually; at first everything shows in dark uncertain shapes; with no colour or shade, but gradually as the light increases all this is added.[32]

Bramwell Booth dealt with the word "our" in Genesis where God said that man was created in our image (Genesis 1:26).

> There were no other forces for Him to commune with, so He communed with Himself. That wonderful unity which we speak of sometimes as the God-head, as God the Father, God the Son, and God the Holy Ghost.[33]

General William Booth, confronted with the biblical controversy of the day, felt compelled to state:

> Mistakes in names and words do not destroy the sense of the main teaching. Misquotations do not interfere with the true meaning. Treating parables as facts, and facts as parables, and the like, does not alter the general trend of the meaning of what is written. Is the story of the Prodigal Son a mind picture or an actual incident? The value of its teaching is not affected either way. Seeming contradictions in the Bible may be explained away by better knowledge; by customs of the age, in which the book was written, or by some incidents that occurred at the time of which, at present, we have no knowledge.[34]

In spite of all the questions being raised by biblical criticism, the Army possessed a determined faith in the literal sense of Scripture as God's own revelation. Any questions regarding it would be answered in time. The literal sense was foundational for understanding God and his relation to the human situation. Mrs. Booth, in a message on Revelation 2:1-5, declared: "... this is a direct message from Christ himself to a company of his own people in a certain state of religious experience ... Hear what He says of them in this second verse . . . ."[35]

Where the Bible presented itself as an historical record, it was accepted as such by the Army in those early years. In the doctrine book of 1881, there was a clear statement on human creation.

> God made Adam and Eve, our first parents, perfectly pure, and pronounced them to be good. He also made every arrangement for them to keep on being good and happy, which had they done, the world would now have been full of holy, happy people.[36]

The Army established the literal sense as foundational to its own theology on this passage. Creation was historical as outlined in the Bible and then theological inferences were drawn from the passage. In an article in *The Officer* Booth discussed earthly visits by ghosts and referred to the historicity of Scripture as his authority. He argued that "no one who believes this Bible can deny the reality of the appearance of Samuel when asked for by Saul in the last hour of his despair."[37]

The Bible was not only the final authority for all that the Army taught about God, it was also foundational in the Army's *expression* of that teaching, encouraging the *dramatic nature* of that expression. Mrs. Booth, commenting on Revelation 7:15 in response to critics who called for a very quiet religion as opposed to the noise, especially of The Salvation Army, argued:

> But some of us are getting accustomed to a great noise, we are practising ourselves beforehand in proclaiming His praises anticipatory to that great day when the kingdoms of this so long sin-blighted, sin-cursed world, shall have become the kingdoms of our God and His Christ.[38]

She went on to describe in all probability what the Kingdom of God would be like and then added: "You say, 'Yes, it is a beautiful picture, but, like many others, it is impossible.' Do not say 'impossible,' for God says it SHALL BE."[39]

In other ways Scripture was foundational and authoritative for Army expression. Regarding the Army's missionary work, this argument was voiced:

> It is necessary to counteract the specious philosophy that would leave the heathen in his blindness, on the plea that "he is happy enough as he is." Pernicious in the extreme, such doctrine runs directly counter to the express demand of Christ. It is, moreover contrary to fact.[40]

The rationale for engaging in missionary work rested on Scripture, as in some cases did mission methodology. In a report by Major Tucker on his work in India dated September 7, 1884, he wrote:

> In visiting the villages the instructions of Matthew X, are usually carefully observed—without money, food, change of clothes, or bedding; our Officers trust entirely to the hospitality of the villagers. Usually they get two meals a-day, sometimes only one. Where the people are friendly, and wish to get saved, they stop for some time. When this is not the case, they deliver the message and pass on.[41]

While Scripture did supply example for some Army methodology, the Army made no effort to mimic first-century Christian methods. The Army ascribed to a literal sense of Scripture that prevented it from falling into a narrow literalism. Charles Pratt charged that the Army's form of religion was not the form of the Lord Jesus or the Apostles as they preached the Kingdom. He seemed to imply that apostolic worship as described in Scripture should be reproduced or adhered to in all ages. The early Army unequivocably rejected this premise. The Army found nothing in the literal sense of Scripture that indicated that religious form was biblically confined to any one practice. The Army doctrine book of 1881 raised the question of whether or not the early Christians adopted one particular plan of government. The doctrine book concluded: "No, and, even if they did, it would still be very difficult to prove that, because they followed certain customs, we are in any way under God's commands to do what they did."[42]

Early Army leaders consciously pursued an understanding of the literal sense of Scripture rather than a narrow literalism. As a result Booth could argue that ". . . some undervalue it, and in consequence, neglect to read and to be governed by its teaching; while others OVERESTIMATE it by regarding it as the only way in which God speaks to man."[43] Jannaway discussed The Salvation Army and the Bible and picked up on this statement arguing that

> . . . an over-estimation of the Bible is practically an impossibility, in that we have no Scriptural or other grounds for believing that God *now* speaks to man in any other way than through the medium of that blessed Book.[44]

Blinded by his own literal approach to the writings of Booth, Jannaway was attacking a straw horse. Booth did not oppose the authority of the Bible, advocating that there were other things that spoke of God equally as well as the Bible. The first doctrine of the Army and the entire theology of the Army doctrine book argues against this. Discussing the work of the Holy Spirit himself, expressed through people, the doctrine book argued that this too was a communication of God which ought not to be underestimated.

> It is therefore wrong and misleading to argue that we have no other way of ascertaining the mind of the Spirit concerning our own salvation, or our duty to our fellows, except through the *written* word. And it is one great cause of so much *tame experience* in the knowledge of God, and so much *lame effort* to extend the kingdom of God. The *living, active, positive agency of God* is comparatively shut out of the world, and a dead book placed in its stead.[45]

Booth simply made the point that Scripture was not definitive on the form of worship. He opposed a literalism that would measure all forms of religious expression by how the Apostles worshipped. The same was true of Church government. For the early Army, an interpretation of Scripture that concretized the form of worship to first century expression, rather than allow it to change and become whatever was effective in presenting and expressing God's truth, was a misreading of the literal sense of Scripture.

The early Army would have nothing of a cold, lifeless bibliolatry. Its focus on the literal sense of Scripture helped it to enjoy a freedom that other views lacked. One Army critic charged

> That the Bible generally is reverenced, quoted, and applied, may perhaps be true; but who that has either had much to do with the movement personally, or who has read the various accounts of meetings, the addresses, & c., but must feel that very little of bible teaching is to be found?
> The "sword of the Spirit," though not sheathed, is but little used.[46]

The implication is that testimony should be clearly referenced by specific passage, chapter, and verse(s). The writer argued:

> Is it to the *word of God* brought home with power to his heart and to his conscience? Yes, sometimes; but much more often to a general happy experience of the love of Christ to him, learnt from the detailed experience of another. We, tracing it back to the word of God, know it to be scriptural fact that "God so loved the world that He gave His only-begotten Son, that whosoever believeth in Him should not perish, but have everlasting life," and we rejoice with Him. But on what foundation does the love of Christ to him rest in that convert's soul?[47]

To the early Salvationists, the message of Christian truth and a genuine spiritual experience of that truth were preeminent, rather than an intellectually detailed knowledge of the Bible—book, chapter, and verse. This is not to say that they were ignorant of biblical facts, stories, truths, or even neglected the memorization of Scripture. It is to say that they were free to express their experiences in testimony rather than obliged to prove their biblical acumen.

It is significant that those most concerned about religious form had little appreciation for the dramatic qualities of

Salvation Army worship and preachment. One writer criticized:

> In all that we read of the apostles of our Lord, or of those apostolic men whom God has, in later times, greatly owned in the conversion of souls, one finds nothing akin to the proceedings of these salvationists.[48]

> Have, then, the good old Gospel ways of humility and decency and order gone out of date, and has the dispensation of comicality, irreverence, masquerade, and self-assertion taken the place? Will God no longer bless the preaching of Christ and Him crucified, unless the Gospel is presented in association with what is grotesque and incongruous?[49]

Another author referred to the verbal expression of the Army found in a *War Cry* and wrote:

> . . . one reporter says the meeting was 'boiling over with holy-ghost power' [holy ghost being here an adjective]. Another says: 'The steam was up.' Other strange expressions will be given when I am enabled to verify them accurately.[50]

The writer went on to assert:

> There can be no doubt that, in Salvation Army language, "Holy Spirit," "steam," and the rest to follow, are all synonyms. For the abiding and growing ill effect of *any* corrupt vocabulary, I refer you to Archbishop Trence on "The Study of Words." But we need no such mastermind to point out the *present* evil of introducing a fresh set of coarse, slangy, semi-ludicrous language into the service of a religion whose handmaids, if not *clean*-handed, are better away out of the house altogether.[51]

The narrow literalism expressed above made no allowance for the marked cultural difference between the lower classes and the educated classes of Victorian England. The critics were unable to decipher the literal sense of the theological expression of the poor. As a result they confused authentic expressions of spiritual experiences with their own preconceptions of methodology. They did not understand that the dramatic expression of the Army's theology was not a result of methodology as much as it was religious experience within a different culture. To put it another way, religious experience generated methodology, not vice versa. If questions were to be raised, they should have been raised about experience more than methodology.

In understanding Scripture according to its literal sense, the Army's theological expression was encouraged to be dramatic. The literal sense of Scripture is sensational but not superfically so. Bairstow asserted:

> The ten plagues of Egypt; the dividing of the waters of the Red Sea, the pillar of cloud by day, and a fire by night; the thunders and lightenings of Mount Sinai, the mount altogether in a smoke; the voice of a trumpet exceeding loud and long, and waxing louder and louder; Moses speaking, and the living God answering him by a voice—all this was sensational, but the startling record thrills human hearts still . . . .[52]

Preaching in London on the eve of his departure for New York, there to begin officially Salvation Army operations in the United States, Commissioner Railton declared:

> I do think that the time has come for us to get back again to the good old religion of the Lord Jesus Christ, to the grand old Gospel, which says, "Repent, for the Kingdom of God is at hand;" and which says, "Repent, or be damned;" which goes forth to the nations and says, "We claim you; you have no right to live without Christ; you have no right to reject Christ. It is your duty, and you must submit to your Master or perish to all eternity;" and I thank God we are going forward in the Spirit and in His might to carry on war on that system in the United States, and wheresoever else God shall lead us.[53]

Bramwell, looking back to those early days, wrote:

> . . . it is difficult to see what alternative there is to a militant and aggressive evangelism. If we believe that the issues presented to the soul in this life are so momentous, what else can we do but bring the gospel of salvation as persuasively, as simply, as startlingly, as persistently as we can before the minds and consciences and hearts of men?[54]

The Army took literally the doctrine of sin with its hell and eternal punishment, as well as redemption through Christ. The *London Times* noted:

> The Doctrines of the Salvation Army, briefly stated are, "Utter ruin grew through the fall; salvation alone, from first to last, through the atonement of Christ, by the Holy Spirit; the great day of judgment, with its reward of heaven for ever for the righteous and hell for ever for the wicked."[55]

In discussing the name change from The Christian Mission to The Salvation Army, Booth wrote:

> There is a hell. A hell as dark and terrible as is the description given of it by the lips of Jesus Christ, the truthful. And into that hell men are departing hour by hour. While we write men are going away into everlasting punishment.[56]

Railton took the reality of Hell one step further. He wrote:

> The eternal fire instead of being a horrible exaggeration as the devil tries to make men think, is a most feeble attempt to explain the horrors of that hatred that will search out every hidden spot and fill the whole being with agony.[57]

Catherine Booth believed in a literal battle between good and evil. Bramwell recounts:

> Her whole life was a triumph over foes seen and unseen. This was no sham fight for her, no spectacular tournament. There was no need to summon up imaginary enemies. Here was the enemy present in very truth. Catherine Booth was intensely aware of evil.[58]

"There were times when she thought, and said, that the Devil reserved some of his most venomous darts for her, that she had been singled out for his special malice."[59] John Lawley, one of the Army's earliest commissioners and the man who conducted many of the Founder's services of invitation after the message had been delivered, was acutely aware of a real devil, a real hell, and the battle between the powers of darkness and light. Bramwell Booth tells of John Lawley in one of his unpublished messages. As a boy, after lying,

> John's conscience so troubled him, that he dreamed that the Devil put a ladder up to the window of the room in which he slept, and looking in said, "You belong to me. I know you

do, because you told a lie. I've come to fetch you." The little lad awakened in a frenzy of terror, and, as he shivered in the darkness, vowed to God that he would never tell another lie.[60]

Lawley never lost this sense of a literal hell and the reality of a spiritual battle going on for the souls of men. He described a Salvation Meeting in Amsterdam in this way:

> Lovers of souls were stationed in every part, a great battle was in progress, the armies of Heaven and Hell had met face to face; the fight was a hand-to-hand one; to lose was damnation, but to win was Salvation.[61]

Indeed, this belief in a spiritual war between good and evil and the reality of sin and hell, as well as holiness and heaven, made for powerful drama. It was this drama that gave the Army its *raison d'etre*. Booth asserted:

> The world, this very world, including this very England which never ceases boasting of its freedom, is sold under sin, held in slavery by Satan, who has usurped the place and power and revenues of Jehovah, and who is indeed its lord and master, and to deliver it and fulfill to the very letter the Master's command, an army of deliverance, of redemption, of emancipation is wanted.[62]

The dramatic form of Army literature was rhetorical and inspirational, rather than methodical and rationalistic. Resting on the literal sense of Scripture, it conjured up in the mind's eye dynamic, dramatic images. Imagine in your own mind's eye a world dying in sin, in poverty, in sickness and degradation, and an Army marching with trumpet and drum and flags flying, to vanquish evil and save the lost. This is exactly what the early Salvationists imagined, not only when they read Scripture or closed their eyes in prayer, but also when they looked around themselves. Even more than Ezekiel who had a vision of bones being clothed with flesh and new life, the early Salvationists saw an Army of real people like themselves, raised up and marching forward and that dramatic expression was motivated by the literal sense of Scripture.

Bairstow implied that the dramatic power of the literal sense of Scripture could change human hearts and human behavior. He reported that

> ... when Savonarola took as his theme the mystical visions of the Apocalypse, which he applied with terrible directness to the frightful evils of that immoral age, he drew upon himself the bitter hatred of the clerics; but Divine inspiration was attributed to him by the people. Under the impulse of the popular enthusiasm which the earnestness of the prophet engendered, women flocked in troops to the public squares to fling down their costliest ornaments, and the gay gallants and grave scholars publicly consigned to the flames before the gates of the cathedral filthy and licentious literature in armfuls.[63]

Booth and the early Army believed in the power of the literal message of Scripture to change lives because the literal sense of Scripture presented a God who was alive and involved in the human predicament of sin. In Railton's biography of Booth, a sordid picture of life in the East End of London is painted. He described the squalid misery and ungodliness all around and then discussed the faith the Booths must have had to believe that God could and would work in this pit of hell. Railton drew his conclusions from Scripture itself.

> ... we cannot but see in the whole matter the hand of God Himself fulfilling His great promise: "Even the captives of the mighty shall be taken away, the prey of the terrible shall be delivered, for I will contend with them that contend with thee, and I will save thy children. And all flesh shall know that I the Lord am thy Saviour, and thy Redeemer, the Mighty One of Jacob."[64]

For the Army in its formative years, the Bible embodied within human flesh was the means of the salvation of the world.

> We contend that the way to save the world is by the living testimony of living witnesses filled with the Holy Ghost, who speak because they love to speak, who became so identified with their Saviour on His Cross that their life is guided by the

171

same motive as His was, that is absolute self-abnegation, and constant, unwearying effort to persuade men to turn from idols to serve a living, loving God.

Jesus said to His witnesses, "Go and TELL THE GOOD NEWS to all nations."[65]

When Scripture becomes so embodied in human lives there is present the most powerful, dramatic expression possible. What is drama, what is art in all of its forms, except a description of life? It is taking life as one sees it and then interpreting what is seen and felt through an art form. So the foundational basis of all art, of all drama is in some aspect, life. When we look at life itself and find that it depicts a knowledge of God, then this is dramatic theological expression. The Salvation Army exhibited a dramatic expression of Scripture as it endeavored to embody that understanding, live it out, and so communicate it to the world.

This old reading of Scripture, combined with a most colorful expression of ministry, brought the Scriptures to life among a most needy and in some cases a most heathen and despicable segment of society. It helped to awaken a word culture from its preoccupation with form, order, and propriety to the truth that people are more complex and react to a far greater assortment of stimuli than the stimulus of Bentham's one-principle utilitarianism. Even more, it argued that God, rather than prescribing in minute detail what was acceptable worship, was far more tolerant of the peculiarities of human nature and far more approving of genuine, non-traditional spirituality than many supposed. In this it helped many of those disfranchised to regain a sense of purpose for their future. In addition to finding a place to belong—a home so to speak—they found a hope; they did have some influence on the future before them.

Chapter XII

A Dramatic Expression of Theology in Human Life

The dramatic theology of The Salvation Army was a life-centered theology of the most practical variety. As such, it appealed to the culture of the masses, a culture that had a concept of life quite different from Victorian ideals.

In the industrial age of Victorian England, people were learning to work and to play. As the economy improved, more people could play. More time for playing as well as more things to play came into being. Philosophically, this word culture implied that reality lay outside a person in things and events. The key concept became "doing". Work was a means to happiness, but happiness came by doing as much of life as possible. Today we work for retirement so that we can do all the things we could not do while we were working.

In an image-oriented culture the key concept is "being." Here reality is located within the person. The world is important as it contributes to the enrichment and development of one's personhood. This was the cultural context to which the early members of the Army were more suited. In a day when work and play were opposites to many people, these soldiers were finding pleasure and deep joy in the work of this movement. For them work and play were not so distinct, and since their work was a source of real joy, even though unlearned, they were very teachable. Walter Ong ascribed this relationship of work, play, and learning to a pre-word or oral culture. He wrote:

> In an oral culture, verbalized learning takes place quite normally in an atmosphere of celebration or play. As events, words are more celebrations and less tools than in literate cultures. Only with the invention of writing and the isolation of the individual from the tribe will verbal learning and understanding itself become "work" as distinct from play, and the pleasure principle be downgraded as a principle of verbalized cultural continuity.[1]

For the early Salvationists the practice of their faith was a way of life that brought great joy and satisfaction.

Life-centered theology has been a characteristic concern of Army literature from its early mission days. No instance of theology being discussed for theology's sake was found in this study; there was no delving into abstract notions. Everything written was related to the Army's program and purpose for being and was illustrated by real characters engulfed in depravity or ministering to the depraved. In print, the picture of the Christian life was shown over and over again. *The East London Evangelist* of 1869, a forerunner of Army periodicals, was filled with human-interest stories intended to encourage or to teach or to inspire.[2] In *all* of the early publications of the Army, people could *see* success stories and they could *see* the results of sin not only in present troubles and tragedies but in eternal condemnation. Salvation Army publications have never lost this person-centered perspective.

The main emphasis of Army theology was simply that persons could be changed from sinners to saints through the power of God. This was presented through biographical accounts *showing* the sin, sorrow, and beastliness of life before conversion, and the hope, love, and purpose of life after conversion. In Railton's book *Heathen England*, chapter 10 is titled "Soldiers in Hospital." This chapter gave nothing but glowing reports of Christians facing death.

> Here lies a young man dying of consumption. "Never mind," says he to a visitor one day; "I shall be in heaven soon. I shall never be with you at class; but tell them, 'We shall gather at the river,'" Told of some of the dying words of a former Army associate, he exclaims, "Bless God! I shall see him soon."[3]

How do soldiers of Christ die?

> Desperate trust; not only a quiet peace that death itself could not shake; but a triumph far surpassing all the triumphs of life—such have been the experience of many an Army death-bed.[4]

Throughout *Heathen England*, personal illustrations undergird the points Railton makes. This is dramatic expression more than rational discourse. We are confronted with experience rather than doctrine.

In this emphasis on people the theology of God is interpreted through man. Bramwell Booth testified that ". . . from the first days of my officership I saw religion to be essentially practical, not a matter of theory and theology only, but of life and conduct."[5] God was to be seen and judged by his influence in the world as seen in his people. As Jesus showed the Father to the world, Christians were to show Jesus to the world.

The most powerful force in early Army expression, and that which more than anything else made that theological expression dramatic, was the emphasis laid upon the living dramas that comprised The Salvation Army and its work. Without question, the most powerful of those living dramas was the Founder himself. Evans, discussing the Victorian Age, wrote: "The Army . . . ideals were so vividly embodied in the visible presence and character of 'The General' as to be unshakeable."[6]

For some, the Army's dramatic expression of theology was lost in its practical ministry to people in need. Governor Waite of Colorado praised Booth with these words. "'You, my dear General, recognize poverty as the arch foe of Christianity. You would give the poor man bread instead of a tract.'"[7] This was an accurate observation but secular in interpretation. There was, however, a dramatic interpretation of this work, theological in nature and much more befitting the Army spirit. As far as Booth was concerned, it was and always would be sin that was the arch foe, not only of the poor but also of the rich and the in-between. Booth sought to bring Jesus Christ to the poor, clothed in the flesh of every soldier and officer in The Salvation Army, that they might convey to the poor the "living bread" of heaven. Professor Watson Smith saw this in Booth's social scheme.

> The Darkest England Scheme is but an outward embodiment and manifestation of Him who died and rose again in the carrying out of that grand scheme in Judaea and Jerusalem. The Spirit of the Lord was upon Him and had annointed Him. The powers of darkness and unbelief prevailed against the outward form, but the Spirit rose again. That Spirit has now risen in England, and is present in the Darkest England Scheme of The Salvation Army, and in all similar schemes animated by that Spirit. The Spirit of Jesus Christ now walks the streets of London and those of our great cities; is present in the slums, the Shelters, the Elevators; speaks peace to the converts at their lowly meetings, and gives sight to many who are blind among the poor, needy and suffering.[8]

Bramwell Booth declared in 1906:

> Well, we recognise that the battle for Christ is lost or won, so far as the working classes are concerned, not in the arena of Church life, or in the debating club, or in the public press, but on the working man's own battle-field—the workshop. Far too much importance is attached to the argument of the lip and the pen. A thousand Clarions and a thousand Blatchfords are powerless before clean living and unselfish devotion to the service of others in the spirit of Jesus Christ.[9]

To those filled with an anxiety that seemed to defy resolution, the Army held out a hope that could be seen and felt. People were reaching out to people in a way that brought their spirits into dynamic relationship with each other.

> It was an enthusiastic religion that swallowed them up, and made them willing to become wanderers and vagabonds on the face of the earth—for His sake to dwell in dens and caves, to be torn asunder, and to be persecuted in every form.[10]

Some churchmen agreed that the unchurched masses had to be met on their own ground but had different ideas of how this was to be accomplished. Canon F.W. Farrar, rector of St. Margaret's, Westminster, proposed the establishment of brotherhoods of clergy who would live together celibately and work at the invitation of the parish clergy.

> ... Farrar explained that he put his hope in brotherhoods because the Church had 'practically lost all effectual hold on the mass of the working classes,' and because he could see no other way to regain such a hold than to form communities of priests trained and dedicated to doing among the masses what the parish clergy could not do.[11]

Here the answer was still with the clergy. The great need was more and uniquely qualified clergymen.

Not all in the Church of England believed that the answer rested solely or even primarily in the clergy. There were those, who, like Booth and the Army, saw the importance of lay involvement. An ex-Salvation Army officer, H.A. Colville, organized the Lichfield Evangelist Brotherhood in 1887. This was a body of laymen trained as evangelists who assisted parish priests. Wilson Carlile, believing The Salvation Army had provided a worthy example of the effectiveness of lay ministry, organized the Church Army, which consisted of recruits from the Church, a kind of special Church force. While effective, it was controlled by the Church and significantly different from the Army. Inglis quoted Charles Booth regarding this difference.

> The Salvation Army . . . is before everything a religious community. The Church Army is not a separate religious body at all; it is merely a working association of members of the Church of England.[12]

Inglis concluded: "Lacking thus the peculiar fellowship which nurtured the enthusiasm of the Salvation Army, the Church Army was bound to be less spectacular."[13] The peculiarity of the Army fellowship existed because of Booth's radical concept of the relationship of layman and cleric. The heart and mind of Booth regarding this subject is revealed in one of his letters.

> The idea never dawned on me that any line was to be drawn between one who had nothing else to do but preach and a saved apprentice lad. . . . I have lived, thank God, to witness the separation between layman and cleric become more and more obscured, and to see Jesus Christ's idea of changing in a moment ignorant fisherman into fishers of men nearer and nearer realisation.[14]

Booth brought his lay people so completely into the salvation ministry of the Army that one writer reported of Booth: "He directs and controls the preaching of 15,393 evangelists, of whom 645 are paid 'officers.'"[15]

The Army provided much more than something to which its converts could belong. The Salvation Army was a way of life, an "enthusiastic" way of life expressed in community action. Reverend Wyndham Heathcote, a former Salvation Army officer, brought out this idea of community as opposed to the individualism of a nineteenth-century, word culture. "The Salvation Army appears to me to have arisen in the providence of God by way of contrast to, and reaction from, the reign of individualism."[16] Heathcote clarified his point.

> . . . all social views of Christianity were lost, and the individual became all in all. The salvation of the individual as an individual, the rights of the individual, the privileges of the individual, were being pressed beyond measure, so that we

were beginning to forget that we are essentially and by our very nature not merely individuals, but social beings; and we were ignoring the fact that Christianity regards us as such. Every man was beginning to do what was right in his own eyes, and own no master but his own self-will.[17]

Heathcote asserted:

Salvationism, as existing amongst the officers and rank and file . . . has resuscitated the idea that becoming a Christian involves becoming a member of a community and that he only acts truly to himself who acts as a member of that community.[18]

A word culture dominated by reason is the realm of the thinker, the *individual*. An image-oriented culture dominated by the emotion is the realm of the community. The dramatic nature of the Army's theological expression was underscored by its community life. Heathcote argued that for the Army to remain consistant to its idea of community it should have come into full harmony with the Church.[19] However, the Army was more in harmony with a feudal community than with a social theory of the Church. It saw itself living in a hostile world, not only distinct from the masses but also from dead churches, a lonely bastion surrounded by and in spiritual warfare with the powers of evil. Reverend Cannon Scott Holland discussed how to reach the masses by using the Army as an example.

These excellent people are a standing proof that large masses of the people can only be met by (one) simple evangelical fervour; (two) outdoor processions; (three) a ministry chosen from these poorer classes which are practically still refused a vocation in the Church of England.[20]

What Mr. Holland observed in the Army was a dramatic expression of theology through the individual and community life that was the Army. It consisted of fervor, a visible Army marching and working in full sight of the public and comprised of the most common people of society. This was a community with a purpose, an "excellent people" who were a "standing proof" of how to reach the masses with the Gospel.

There is a theological term, the "priesthood of the believer," already discussed in Chapter VIII, that adequately describes this new community expression, both in its self-understanding and its methodology. The Salvation Army understood that God called all of his people to the vocation of priests with all of the divine authority and responsibilities assigned to that position. It was this radical sense of the priesthood of the believer whereby the laity shared an equal responsibility with the clergy for the salvation of the lost, that made The Salvation Army revolutionary and dramatic. It was revolutionary in its acceptance of the laity for the ultimate work of the kingdom and dramatic because an Army of clergy and laity came into being for all the world to *see*. As in *all* of the early literature of the Army, people could *see* success stories of conversion as well as the tragedies of sin, so in human lives and the corporate action of this new movement could people behold a drama of theological expression.

While the Army was the only new denomination of national and international dimensions to come out of Victorian England, it was not alone in its dramatic theological expression. Charles Spurgeon was filling his church in London at this time. He was described as natural, simple, highly dramatic, and manifestly in earnest, when preaching the doctrines of the Gospel.[21] According to our source, his sermons were "highly dramatic" presentations.

> Everything lives, moves, and speaks in his sermons. The whole discourse, indeed, is only a series of pictures, brought vividly before the audience. There are no cold and dry abstractions. [Ever] truth is clothed with life and power. Metaphors and similes crowd upon one another....[22]

The writer set the earnestness of Spurgeon into a powerfully dramatic context.

> He seems to put his whole soul into every sermon. He

speaks as if he stood with his audience upon a trembling point between heaven and hell. His great desire evidently is to do God's work well, and save as many souls as he can. Hence the directness of application, the fervid, hortatory style, which rivets the attention, forces home the truth, and makes every hearer feel himself personally addressed by the preacher.[23]

In the Army's dramatic theological expression, there was a place for the sensational. The Army was bent on catching the attention of segments of society not only alienated from religion but caught up in the most depraved expressions of social and moral degradation possible. Sensational events and stunts, even in their most crude forms, were, at times, used to attract attention. One of the more bizarre stunts uncovered in this study was used to justify this methodology.

> Yet who dare again say anything against even these measures when one has heard how Commissioner Frank Smith—one of the most successful of all the salvationists pioneers in America—gained, in his captaincy days, the attention of the Liverpool roughs when other efforts had failed? He mounted a charger, and riding with his face towards the animal's tail through the street, entered the barracks *riding on to the platform*. By this singular procedure he never wanted for an audience, but won crowds of fallen men and women for God and heaven.[24]

Sensational stunts like this ought not to be passed off judgmentally as base and vulgar. They were appropriate and necessary for the cultural context to which they were directed. The Primitive Methodists, in 1879, wrote of the Army:

> Truth, presented in an "orderly, dignified, and orthodox manner," did not touch the people, and, to arrest them, it was determined to accommodate the truth to the condition and needs of those who must otherwise remain outside the circle of its influence. The adoption of the military system, the simplifying of the Gospel, the employment of women speakers, the parades through the streets with music and singing, flags and banners, the intense homeliness of the services, the character of the buildings used, and all the paraphernalia of the Army have answered a Divine purpose.[25]

Another writer discussed opposition or support for the Army and focused on its military organization.

> When men in masses were sunk into the condition of their lowest classes, there was but one hope for them—the action of some organization which would win the individual by a sympathy of discipline and numbers, by appealing to the imagination, by some special bond of union. There was a remarkable fitness with the military idea to reach some people. It favoured the idea of a *sudden* change in their lives, their only chance of amendment; it immediately supplied the moral force required to aid the weak volition of the convert, and then it trained him under a regular system of discipline and instruction.[26]

The editor of *The Month* charged that the Army's ". . . utter want of reverence, its appeals to excited feelings, its absence of any solid foundation of truth, exclude it from things Divine. It is of the earth, earthy."[27] The Army was earthy. It was in touch with human life at its most expressive and, often, its rawest point. Bairstow, after reading the definition of sensation in Chambers's Dictionary, wrote of the Army's method:

> "Now," thought I, "if all this is really true, how else are the poor going to be reached?—nay, indeed, how else have they ever been reached? You cannot reach them through their intellects, for among the adult population the effects of modern educational reform have had no chance of development, and far too many have brains besodden with drink as scarcely even to be able to understand twenty consecutive sentences."[28]

Where traditional symbols of God and Church were rendered ineffective, new symbols came alive in the Army. They were earthy and perhaps radical, but they caught the eye and the heart of the poorer classes. Railton declared: "Our cathedral is the open air, our college is the prayer-room, our library the Bible, our sanctuary the theatre, our diplomas the blackguards turned into preachers at our services."[29] The uniform and the Army flag became two of the most visual and powerful symbols of the Army. To many outside the Army, the uniform especially became a symbol of caring. A writer in the *War Cry* of 1890 tells of his experience when stopped by someone so weighed down with problems that he was about to do away with himself.

> I inquired what motive he had in selecting me to speak to, when he replied that he knew our uniform indicated that we belonged to the Lord, and trembling from head to foot, and with large tears in his eyes, he inquired if there was such a thing as hope for a poor degraded human being like me.[30]

Symbols such as these set a new priority on a person's imaginative nature. By far the most powerful symbol was the concept of an Army itself. The message of this new movement preached a new way of life inaugurated by instantaneous conversion. It demanded pure living and provided a program which had a place and a ministry for every convert. The symbol of an Army was ideally suited to this message. Both conveyed the same notions.

Salvation Army expression gave rise to mental pictures of what its message and ministry were all about. It was this dramatic side of the Army, treating the emotions as legitimate, that made its impact upon society from the first. In a leading article, *The Times* described the expression of Salvation Army religion.

> The "Salvation Army," as far as it can be known to the uninitiated, consists of bands of men marching through the streets, . . . with banners, devises, and sometimes emblematic helmets and other accoutrements, singing sensational hymns, and by their gestures inviting all whose eyes they succeed in catching to fall in and march with them to some headquarters or rendezvous of those that are to be saved.[31]

There was no report of what the Army was saying, only how it was saying it. This did not mean that the Army was saying nothing. A look at the numbers of books, magazines, and newspaper and periodical articles that were produced from the Army's beginnings, even in its mission days, impresses one that the Army had much to say. But what it said was straightforward evangelical theology. How it said it was another matter.

Salvation Army expression caused writers to report in mental images its events. One reporter wrote:

> Shortly after 7 o'clock last evening a "squad" under the command of a captain who at intervals blew a trumpet, a "call to sinners," were perambulating the streets of Bermonsey preparatory to proceeding to the "Salvation Factory" to "find peace. "The processionists, as usual, went along singing hymns, and were preceded by a couple of youths armed with a long pole, from which were suspended a couple of naphtha lamps lighted, such as were used by street traders at night to display their wares on their barrows.[32]

Another writer said specifically: "There is just one other point on which I should like to touch, in order to complete the mental picture with which Salvationism has impressed me."[33]

Victorian England was quite familiar with armies and navies reaching around the world to colonize that world for the Queen and mother England. As a result, the common people could understand the notion of an Army of God reaching into the whole world in an effort to win that world for the heavenly King and make it the Kingdom of God. Even more, these people saw that Army marching, heard it playing and speaking, read of its invasions throughout London, then the United Kingdom, and very quickly around the world.

The message of the Army was dramatized on stage, on the street-corners, in front of barrooms, and anywhere else people could be gathered, and many found in it a place seen by the eyes of the heart and mind, a place as a musician or a penitent-form sergeant, perhaps as a slum sister, certainly as an open-air soldier. Whatever the position, the role was readily identified.

That role combined with a fervent spiritual commitment and motivated by a personal, individual experience with God himself, added an inner conviction and assurance that brought a vision of meaning, purpose, and fulfillment to the ministerial concern. That inner substance was an inner conviction rooted in the message of Salvation for the world. It dominated and set the parameters of the Army's methodology.

The Army's sober understanding of this cause prevented just the sensationalism of which it was criticized. Booth writing in the days of the Christian Mission gave this direction to his missioners.

> Refuse to do or allow anything to be done which is not in accordance with the Spirit and which does not square with the aim of the Mission. Beware of new and sensational schemes. Resolutely keep out all worldly stratagems for attracting attention or obtaining money. Stick to the old ways of the Mission. Keep the principles and object for which it was first originated ever before your eyes, and strive continually to make your branch of it a living exemplification thereof.[34]

It was this "inner substance" that kept the Army's theological expression essentially dramatic, rather than sensational and accounted for its success. While there was power in methodology, it was *not* simply methodology to which the Army owed its success. The methods of the Army were never primary, and for this reason the sensationalism of those methods never gained the preeminent place in the Army's theological expression. Bramwell asserted: "The methods were always secondary to the spirit of enthusiasm and love which prompted any method whereby that spirit might express itself."[35] The methods, whatever they might have been, were subservient to the inner conviction of Salvationists. The methods always clothed the spirit of Salvationism. Bramwell, quoting his mother, put it this way: ". . . the exuberance, the noise, the laughter of a Salvation gathering is not a putting on but a letting out."[36]

The "letting out" was a reasonable expression of the

experience within. Booth would avoid sensationalism but never *spirit*, genuine spirit derived from genuine experience. He said to his missioners:

> When the bones are stirring, bone coming to bone, there will ever be a great noise. So it was in the great excitement of Pentecost. And such excitement, wisely guided, is as salutary as it is natural, and instead of hindering ultimately promotes the work of grace.[37]

The key words in the above quote are "wisely guided." That which undergirded sensational methods was a strong, clear, and fundamental articulation of Christian faith. While the methods of The Salvation Army would be looked upon later as sensational, Booth and the early leaders of the Mission laid a foundation on which the original principles of soul-winning held by the Mission were maintained by The Salvation Army. This sober understanding of mission is declared by Railton, in *Heathen England*. "We confess that we have not the slightest inclination, if we had the power, to place upon the stage of any theatre a mere human performance to draw the people and tickle their fancy."[38]

> We will not go on to the theatre stage, or anywhere else, with anything but Christ and Him crucified, and if that will not draw sufficiently, then we will rest content with whatever audiences we can get.[39]

It was this clear sense of orthodoxy which helped to keep the movement from burning out or breaking up into countless splinter groups as emotion often dictates. Booth recounted a conversation with Cardinal Manning:

> . . . the Cardinal remarked that he thought there could be no question about the Spirit of God being with me in the movement, for how else, he asked, could I have been kept so far faithful to the great doctrines and principles of Divine Truth, as had been my happy fortune.[40]

This inward fire of the message of Salvation, soberly understood and dramatically expressed, was the soil in which the seeds of self-sacrifice, Christian love, and a commitment to world evangelism at any cost, rooted. There was a place for the sensational, but it was never allowed to degenerate into a pervading sensationalism. It ever remained a dramatic expression of Salvation theology.

The early leaders of the Army rejected any judgment of irreverence attached to their expression. Mrs. Booth, in replying to criticisms of sensationalism argued that

> The irreverence charged against them was no irreverence of spirit. Those who spoke so much of silent reverence should remember the class of people from which the Salvation Army converts had been drawn, and the life to which they had been accustomed. Besides, she thought there was more scriptural authority for their noise than for the silence of those who criticised them.[41]

The *Times of London* quoted Mrs. Booth on this subject:

> It was rational, it was reasonable, it was philosophical that they should express their feelings, and those who talked of philosophy and logic, while they were forbidding the energies of a mind to express themselves in the channels God had provided, did not know what they were talking about. They wanted the outward expression of the inward fire. They did not believe in the shouting of people who could do nothing else, but those who had prayed, and wept, and suffered imprisonment in this cause might shout til they were hoarse.[42]

Inglis asserted that Cadman, Corbridge, Dowdle, and Lawley, early leaders of the Army, were simply themselves in the way they acted. They put nothing on for show or influence but naturally belonged to a different culture.

> These were people who themselves had failed to find nourishment for the imagination in church or chapel, and who believed that the form of religion they had found satisfying would similarly satisfy others. With minor exceptions they were the only group of Christian evangelists of their time who approached working-class non-worshippers at their own cultural level.[43]

The *Church Quarterly Review* of 1882 recognized this cultural difference but had little appreciation for it.

The prayers, such as they are, are generally a volley of passionate ejaculations, like "Lord, save souls; save somebody just now; shake sinners over the pit of fire," repeated incessantly, like cries of an Eastern dervish, and accompanied by a violent flinging of the body to and fro; and usually the effect is neither more nor less spiritual or Christian than with the dervishes.[44]

It is significant that the author likens Army praying to the expression of Eastern religions. Eastern culture was basically image rather than word oriented. Booth, talking with Mr. Gladstone, prime minister of England, revealed an interesting glimmer of cultural distinction when he commented on how the Roman Catholics saw the Army. "They consider us, I thought, to have much in common with Francis of Assisi or perhaps Madame Guyon and the mystic class of Religionists."[45] These people represented a contemplative group of religionists who would be more image rather than word oriented. They were imaginative, mystical, faith oriented. Their lives had a single overriding purpose. That purpose in life was in itself a way of life, and it left little time for anything else. The poorer classes were much more in touch with the imaginative mystic whose life was caught up in visions than the utilitarian materialist bound by notions of respectability. The Army uncovered a need and met that need with a dramatic expression of God alive in man and both at work in the world.

An article reprinted from *The Christian Commonwealth* suggested that the Church might profit from this new religious spirit.

Must they not say that for themselves, steeped to the hips in the cold bath of modern culture, the best thing that could happen to them would be a visitation of some such earnestness of inquiry, conviction, confession, and repentance as were seen in the Salvation Army, and its humble regiments shouting hosannahs to the King of Glory? Just imagine, said the speaker, the educated Christian societies of England visited with such a breath of God's Spirit as had stirred the heavy and turbid depths of their lower classes.[46]

Charles Waller discussed this new spirit in a sermon on Sunday, October 29, 1882.

> There must, indeed, be nutrition in that which is provided as food for the souls of all men—and that nutrition is Christ, the Bread of Life, which sustains and nourishes the souls of all men, whether saints or penitent sinners, whether educated or ignorant men. But the seasoning which is given with a nutriment is different according to the palate to which it is offered. And it is this difference of seasoning which makes the difference between the fare of the one class of men and the other, so that what is palatable and digestible to the one is not equally so to the other.[47]

While Waller correctly distinguished between method and message, he underestimated the difference between the Army's expression and that of the established Church. Seasoning or sensational presentation alone, or even primarily, have not the capacity to produce, for any appreciable time, an ". . . earnestness of inquiry, conviction, confession, and repentance . . . ."[48] Yet, for more than 125 years, these attributes have been aroused and preserved within Salvationists. The difference in Army expression was more extensive than a bit of seasoning. The founder implied this when he said: "We exhibited religion in a way so different from their way and the way of their parsons that they positively abhorred the idea of our being a permanent force . . . ."[49]

The Army's theology expressed in individual and community drama encouraged the primacy of feeling in religious life, even as it was encouraged in a culture more image oriented. This was part of the difference in Army expression that raised opposition. The Editor of the Catholic magazine, *The Month*, found grave fault with the Army's emphasis upon feeling, favoring a more intellectual, reasoned approach to the ministry. He recognized the missionary activity of The Salvation Army and excused his church from any great expression like it because of its background and small numbers. However, he went on to say:

> Yet we certainly might do more if we had a more intense appreciation of the value of souls and a greater horror of sin, and more of the Divine compassion of our Lord, and there is no reason why we should not say to ourselves, as we witness the zeal of the Salvationists, what our Lord said to the Jewish lawyer, with respect to the work done by a Samaritan heretic, "Go thou and do likewise."[50]

The writer seemed to believe that simply delineating the problem and explaining the answer was enough to get his fellow Catholics missionary minded. He charged that Salvation Army beliefs were not based rationally, that its doctrines rested on no basis of truth, natural or supernatural, but simply on sentiment. One became a Salvationist only because of a certain feeling, a response relegated to the baser element of society. The author concluded:

> For this reason Salvationist can never be the religion of educated men. It is all very well for a religion to be the religion of the poor, but it must not contain any elements which give reasonable offence to men of highly-trained and cultivated minds. It must appeal to intellectual men as well as to the ignorant.[51]

What was it that made Army religion inadequate?

> The Salvation Army has adopted the spirit of Revivalism in that its strength is being found mainly in an appeal to feeling. It is under the influence of shouting and music, and beating drums, and girls with tambourines, and rousing addresses, and morbid excitement, and startling experiences, that the process of being "saved" takes place.[52]

Our author insisted that the Catholics avoided this problem.

> The Catholic missioner proclaims the mercy of God, the love of God, the Divine compassion of Jesus Christ, His longing desire that the sinner should be saved, but he speaks to the heart, not to the feelings. He appeals to the hope of Heaven, to the fear of Hell, to the emptiness of earthly things, and to the dread of coming Judgment, but to the feelings, *never*.[53]

It is difficult to imagine how the emotionally charged topics mentioned above could have been handled without touching the feelings. The Army made no such effort.

The preeminence of the emotional nature of man was held by Booth from his youth. Speaking of his early life, he said:

> . . . it is true that my early training was such as brought me into contact with the suffering poor, and my young heart was greatly affected by their trials and poverty. Then my early religious life was at once connected with a powerful outpouring of the Holy Spirit, and altogether my own instincts led me to see what I have already stated, that the experimental side of religion—the experience of the heart, was *the great,* if not the *only* valuable part of it.[54]

The Salvation Army did touch the feeling side of people and many were motivated. It even found a place for feeling in discussing doctrine. Concerning the existence of God, the doctrine book of 1881 presents an argument from "inner conviction." It states: "Because I feel in my own soul that there is a God. I always have felt so, and everybody else feels the same . . . ."[55] Another argument is given from "inner experience." It states: "Because I have felt Him at work in my own soul, pardoning my sins, changing my heart, comforting me in sorrow, and making me joyful in Him."[56] A number of arguments are presented for the divinity of Christ. These arguments, on the whole, are presented from Scripture and deal with Christ's attributes, his work of creation, the government of all being in his hands, his ability to raise the dead and judge the world, and the worship of Christ required. All of these rest in Scripture except "proof" 10. The question here is: "Do you have any argument other than from Scripture regarding the deity of Christ?" The answer is "Yes; I argue from my own feelings of what Jesus Christ is to me as a Saviour that He is Divine, and in every way worthy of my supreme love and worship and service."[57] In discussing the doctrine of Holiness, it is stated:

> Yes; we think that all Christians will admit that in those

moments when they realise the greatest nearness to God they feel the strongest urgings of the Spirit to present their bodies a living sacrifice, holy and acceptable unto God.[58]

The primacy of the heart is brought out subtly by Railton, who discussed the purpose of the first training home for would-be officers.

> It was never sought to make these places of intellectual instruction, but rather of soul-culture, where those who did not seek only God's glory and the salvation of souls might be separated from the rest of the candidates by trial under the severe tests of East London toil, and where the truly devoted might be taught how to obtain victory over every possible difficulty.[59]

A dramatic expression of theology is confrontational. When The Salvation Army came to town, the people could see, hear, and, even more, *feel* religion. This was one of the stated objectives of evangelistic preaching given in the Army's periodical *All The World:* "Make them feel their need of it; that is, you must open their eyes, and make them understand something about SIN and DEATH, and JUDG-MENT and HELL."[60] One writer observed a young teenage daughter of an Army Captain who lead a song and then expounded upon the sufferings of Christ on the cross. He wrote: "In what she said, as in her manner of saying it, there was, or what comes practically to the same thing, there seemed to me to be, a certain pathos, and she seemed to feel what she said."[61]

To a great extent it was this pursuit of feeling that brought a power of persuasion into the Army movement. One woman filled with prejudice against the Army, attended a meeting, and was converted to Christ. Her testimony gives evidence of the power in this emphasis on feeling.

> . . . the Army, as represented by its Boston leaders, shows forth that power. You feel it. You *must* feel it. Simple, broken words; uncouth diction, rude grammar, and undue absence or presence of aspirates; nevertheless, back of it all, under it all, through it all, you feel God.[62]

Samuel Logan Brengle, along with his wife, Elizabeth, was touched by this sense of divine presence within the early Salvationists. Mr. Brengle had left a very successful ministry in America to journey to England to offer himself to the General for service in The Salvation Army. He was the first American officer to reach the rank of Commissioner, a rank superseded only by the generalship itself. In 1890, his wife wrote an article for *All The World.* Her topic was "Why am I a Salvationist?" She wrote:

> A certain pure, exalted look marked the face of each uniformed Salvationist, their eyes shone with a calm, holy light—we came afterwards to call it "the Salvation look"—and, as they went on to pray and exhort, their simple speech—though unlearned and provincial—held us with irresistible power. They spoke from an overwhelming personal conviction, and their words, otherwise feeble, carried with them all its weight.[63]

"Such lives as I saw in their faces do not grow in a day's time, nor are they written by a passing emotion, and the evidence of both life-lines and eyes—'where shows the heart'—corroborated the spoken testimony."[64] That which brought the greatest persecution in the beginning was just the characteristic which established the Army in the hearts of its first converts, then in the hearts of her countrymen, and ultimately in the hearts of many of the people worldwide. Even some not at all sympathetic to Army theology believed that the power of the movement lay in its dramatic expression. An atheist declared:

> Their success is due, in my opinion, to four things.
>
> (1) Thorough earnestness.
>
> (2) Unselfish devotion to a noble cause.
>
> (3) The inculcation of a sublime morality.
>
> (4) Dramatic preaching. In each of these respects I think they far surpass other Christian sects.[65]

The writer made no mention of what the Army was teaching, but rather how it was expressing its message. The writer listed attributes whose primary appeal was to the emotion.

While this emotion was considered by many to be vulgar and irreverent, the Army drew different conclusions.

> Now, what makes the difference between these two classes of religionists? They profess to believe in the same truths, and yet their practise is entirely different.

> The only solution seems to be that to the one the Salvation of God is a great REALITY, which, having been accepted, has changed them into new creatures, with new ideas, new motives, new aims, while to the other it is a mere THEORY intellectually accepted indeed, but with little power upon the heart or life.[66]

The Army believed that the inability of the established Church to change lives resulted from its insistence that Christianity was primarily a rational experience and that emotion was secondary and very low. Through an emotional encounter the Army endeavored to make the head receptive to its message in order that the heart might be opened to receive a fullness of spiritual life. It was the heart with its array of emotions that determined spiritual experience, that motivated the will to change. Head knowledge was preparation for heart experience. In *The Officer*, these instructions are given to the Field Officer.

> In every meeting the F.O. should endeavour to deal with both sides of man's nature, that is, with both head and heart. Something should always be addressed to the reason, some explanation of the why and the wherefore of things, and in every meeting there should be an appeal to the heart. That is, the F.O. should make the sinner see that he is wrong, and then appeal to his feelings to induce him to act upon what has been made plain to him.[67]

It was the will of man that needed to be reached and changed, and while the will was reached at the emotional level, it went much deeper than feeling. This distinction can be illustrated if we consider the alcoholic. Many times an alcoholic's feelings are touched with remorse and guilt over his problem. Many affirmations are made to quit drinking, most to no avail, until the one affirmation that works. In this instance, something seems to reach down more deeply than ever before to touch a resolve-of-will issuing in deliverance. The early Army found a way to reach down deeply to this resolve-of-will.

One of the most effective means of reaching that will was in the Church service or the "Meeting" as it is called in the Army. In its formative years the Army possessed a vital sense of worship. It was in the Meeting that the heart was approached, salvation offered, and holiness encouraged. Railton reported on the way the Army taught holiness.

> These phrases were familiar to all English people; but, that their real meaning might not only be taken in but kept ever before his people, The General had established two weekly Holiness Meetings in the Mission Halls, one on Sunday morning and the other on Friday evening. These practises, kept up wherever the Army has gone all these forty-seven years, have resulted in the cultivation of ideals far above those usual even in the most Christian circles.[68]

It was in the Meeting more than anywhere else that head and heart were brought together. If the Army had confronted emotion alone, its expression would have been pure sensationalism. If the Army had confronted reason alone, it too would have become coldly intellectualistic. But the Army's dramatic expression of theology brought head and heart together in true drama comprised of both reason and emotion.

In the formative years of the Army, the primacy of preaching was absolutely recognized in the worship meeting. However, psychologically, spiritually, in many cases unconsciously, the focus of the Meeting was upon the Mercy-Seat. Here was a place where the presence of God dwelt in a most powerful way, where head and heart, reason and emotion came to grips with each other and with him.

In this public, altar experience, the meaning of repentance was rationally understood. It was ". . . the renunciation of all sin, and the unreserved surrender of the soul to God, which is not only a condition of pardon in the first instance, but of continued salvation all the way through."[69] Repentance was part of the arena of rational decision, an act of man and his free will. Bramwell Booth asserted:

> . . . we make our own repentance. God does not give us repentance: that is a thing we have to do. And we have to make our own choice. There comes a moment when we have to say, "I will serve God"—that is our own part. God cannot do that. He would not do it if he could. That is ours.[70]

However, when the rational is joined to the invitation to the Mercy-Seat as the place to make a decision, and when an instantaneous conversion is sought, whereby God's presence is literally expected to indwell the being of the seeker, then the experience takes on a far more emotional and mystical nature. We are now in the realm of spiritual experience, which transcends the head and goes far deeper than the sensationalism of feelings. We are now talking about a resolve-of-will that constitutes a new and different being, one who the Army believed was of God rather than of the world.

This dramatic expression of theology compelled people to respond with far-reaching commitments. The compelling character of the Army's preachment was illustrated in the lament of a father over the loss of his young daughter to The Salvation Army:

> . . . with respect to my child and to other young persons of whom I have heard, I fear the Army influence has a direct tendency to wean the converts from home associations and interests, under the idea that its work is paramount in importance to all other pursuits and obligations, and even to the known wishes of parents.[71]

He observed

> ... that she was the captive of the Salvation Army; that a
> father's love, a daughter's duty, a sweet home in which there
> was every indulgence and comfort, were not to be set in the
> scale against work in the Salvation Army.[72]

The compelling nature of the Army's theology demanded
this total commitment, for it was understood to be a total
commitment to God himself.

Theology dramatically expressed was a commitment
lived out, an "acting out" of the faith. What was said in the
pulpit and written in periodicals and books was expected to
be translated into human lives. What was translated was
believed to be more than morality or an ethic. It was a
divine presence, God himself. In a world where reality was
assessed to be increasingly more materialistic, tangible,
objective, quantifiable and natural, the Army made a place
for the supernatural as the very essence of reality. It possessed a radical sense of the incarnation of God in the lives
of its people which greatly increased the compelling and
dramatic nature of its message and expression. God not
only came as a man, he came as a babe born of poor people.
His first bed was a foul manger from which animals slob-
bered their food. Such a God could be a friend, an intimate
acquaintance of even common people, without denying his
deity, tarnishing his glory, or diminishing his holiness. It
made God real and at hand, concerned and authoritative.
Commissioner Frank Smith wrote of God:

> ... you will find all amongst the poor, the outcast; amongst
> the unwholesome crowds of vagrants and homeless, shoeless
> ones; and having found the Father, you will find heaven.
> What authority have I for saying this? Christ's own words, "I
> was hungered and ye gave *Me* meat." "Naked, and ye clothed
> *Me*." "A stranger, and ye took *Me* in." Too literal, is it for this
> practical age? Literal, indeed, but a literal truth, as they who
> choose a religion of feeling and theory in place of a religion of
> fact and service, will find to their eternal sorrow, for they shall
> hear Him say, "Inasmuch as ye did it not to the least of these
> My brethren, ye did it not unto Me."[73]

Bramwell Booth observed this intimate sense of God with man as he declared:

> Men and women realised as never before the presence of the Saviour with us, bearing not only our sins, but our sorrows, and that in the darkest hour of life He stands at our side, a Consoler, a very present Help in trouble.[74]

Early Salvationists did not feel compelled to protect God. They were compelled to join him in the trenches of spiritual warfare among the dying wrecks of human society around the world, believing that in this radical incarnation which was still going on through them lay the divine power to save the world. God became so real in their hearts and lives that they shouted it to the world and called that world to join them in their salvation drama. The people of the Army had gone beyond finding a home to a visionary hope for the future.

Chapter XIII

A New People

Nurtured by the seed ground of its social, philosophical, and religious origins, cultivated through the teachings of its theological constructs, and pruned through the dramatic expression of those notions of God and man, a new idea evolved in Victorian England. It was an idea of an Army of God called into service.

The sense of spiritual warfare understood within the Army movement had its beginnings in early mission days. In a mission magazine of 1876, a writer reported:

> After much hesitation and prayer, understanding the awful responsibility of those who undertook the generalship of the Lord's army, having received the call, and not daring to refuse it, I went into the battlefield in the open air at Well Street, Hackney, on the last night in the old year. After a slight attack upon the enemy, we marched off with a victorious shout to our hall, and there, praised the dear Lord!'

This is only one example of many found within the body of a dramatic literature that encouraged the evolution of the concept of a valid Army. Railton recognized this evolutionary character. He wrote:

> The farther we advanced, the more desperate the fight became, and more soldierly was the attitude and the language

of our people. As early as October, 1877, an evangelist had
announced his opening services as "War in Whitby." Calling
himself "Captain Cadman," and, describing the Mission as
"The Hallalujah Army," he had succeeded in gathering the
largest congregation we had had up to that time.[2]

In researching this subject, one of the leading historians of
The Salvation Army asserted that the significant growth of
the movement began with its name change from The
Christian Mission to The Salvation Army.

That name change took place one night when Railton
was writing an article in which he described the Mission as
a volunteer army. Bramwell objected, saying that he was no
volunteer. Booth took the pen, scratched out "volunteer"
and inserted "salvation." One wonders what would have
happened to the movement if "volunteer" had been
allowed to remain. It is indeed probable that this single
change initiated the coming-to-awareness of an essentially
new and different concept of being, an Army of God.

In early mission days the military language was visually
descriptive, but it was still in nature more rhetoric than reality. With the advent of The Salvation Army, the notion of
war became a literal reality and the language became far
more emotionally and dramatically charged. The Salvation
Army was more than a name given to a group of people to
describe their work. It breathed life into the notion of a real
army fighting in a real war. As a result, the name Salvation
Army had a dramatic appeal while a term like "Church
Army" remained only descriptive.

In the first issue of *The Officer*, Booth explained the purpose of the magazine in terms of spiritual warfare. ". . . I shall
be able to tell you all that is in my heart concerning this warfare with the world, the flesh, and the devil, which you
ought to know."[3] "Here we can greet each other; here we can
publish the latest miraculous workings; pray for mightier
outpourings of His Spirit, and help each other to greater

earnestness, industry, and sacrifice in the War."[4] In an unpublished address by General Bramwell Booth, he recalled Commissioner Lawley's attitude regarding a change of appointment.

> After the first wrench of leaving his D.C.ship his eyes were opened to the tremendous responsibility which had been committed to him—that of arousing in young men and women a passion for the Holy War.[5]

He went on to write: ". . . many leading Officers like to recollect that it was Lawley's voice that aroused and called them to leave the trivialities of life for Salvation warfare."[6]

Of the nature of this spiritual warfare, Booth declared:

> *No bloody war spirit*, no pandering to the brutal craving for wholesale slaughter, has polluted our pages. We hate war and all its paraphernalia. A word is enough to the wise. Let us beware, even in our illustrations, lest we seem to pander to, or tolerate, the cruel taste for blood.[7]

However, while this warfare was unlike the old Roman Crusades or the countless other religious wars fought through the centuries, it had a sense of terror and anxiety. Booth wrote:

> . . . we would like you to feel . . . that we . . . stand in spirit at your side where the battle is hottest, the bullets fly thickest, the temptations are direct, defeat seems nearest, darkness is blackest and death itself may stare you in the face. Blessed, precious bloodwashed, fire-baptised comrades . . . we ask only to be made the bridge over which you shall march to higher fields, to glorious warfare, desperate deeds and surest victory.[8]

This notion of an Army with the spirit of holy warfare was the main characteristic of the Army in its formative years. However, there were other notions that enhanced and ultimately gave an essentially different connotation to the term Army.

We have discussed the world-wide consciousness of the Army with respect to its ultimate concern in the doctrines of salvation and sanctification. This world view received its impetus from the notion of a real Army while at the same time challenging that Army with greater concern and more possibilities.

Like the notion of the Army itself, this world vision came to consciousness gradually. As The Christian Mission the boundaries of ministry extended beyond the East End and London. A national consciousness had already developed. Railton, who knew best the spirit of Booth in those earliest of mission days, speculated at what might have gone through his mind as he thought upon the notion of his new army.

> . . . when Almighty God does vouchsafe to us such a clear vision of what He would have us be and do, He also strongly assures us all things needful—of grace and power and patience—for there will be more crosses as well as more crowns. But the magnificent privilege of His commission transcends all. Some such thoughts must have filled the mind of William Booth as once more he found himself standing on the threshold of a wider sphere and with the conduct of an organisation which was framed to embrace not London or the provinces merely, but the whole world.[9]

Railton went on to assert:

> Up to this point he had been graciously led thus far, the Divine Hand guiding him in paths he knew not—oftimes a desert experience, in which he had humbly striven to be obedient; and now on the mount of vision God bids him look towards a Promised Land of service, into which he *shall* be permitted to enter because of belief in Him. This is the true story of the inception of The Salvation Army.[10]

With the advent of The Salvation Army, the mission of world conquest became a conscious goal. At the February 1880 departure meeting for Commissioner Railton and his contingent of Salvationist lassies bound for the United States, Mrs. Booth declared:

> The decree has gone forth that the kingdoms of this world shall become the kingdoms of our Lord and of His Christ, and that He shall reign whose right it is, from the rivers to the ends

of the earth. We shall win. It is only a question of time. I
believe that this movement is to inaugurate the great final
conquest of the Lord Jesus Christ.[11]

The Salvation Army's eschatological dogmatism did not go
further than the conviction that the Army was to play a
leading role in this conquest of the world for Christ. Booth
and his Army believed in a coming, real reign of God upon
earth, whereby all people would know him and obey him.
"God will be King, not only in theory, but in practice. He
will not only reign, but govern. The will of God will be the
law of earth, as it is the law of heaven."[12] But the millennium
was not a concern to be belabored except as motivation to be
about God's business of soul-winning. Booth, ever the evangelist and activist, wrote:

> Some say that the general triumph of godliness will be ush-
> ered in by the personal reign of Christ. We Salvationists, how-
> ever, expect it to be preceded by further and mightier out-
> pourings of the Holy Ghost than any yet known, and reckon
> that the war will, thereby, be carried on with greater vigor,
> although, in substance, on the same lines as those on which
> the Apostles fought and died. About these things, however,
> we have neither time nor disposition to argue. Enough for us
> to know that there is a very general concurrence of opinion
> that there is a good time coming . . . .[13]

Salvationists were determined to be part of these "mightier outpourings of the Holy Ghost." With Bible in hand and
heart, many went out from the United Kingdom to the
remotest corners of the world to plant the Army flag. Those
who did not go were asked to give financially and sacrifical-
ly to the cause. In a "Council of War" at Exeter Hall, it was
reported that Booth

> . . . demanded from his army a collection in aid of the work
> of "saving the world." He intimated that he expected to obtain
> L1,000 at that meeting, and he called upon the flock to sub-
> scribe not only their money, but their valuables.[14]

The Army was made up of working-class people and not

a few paupers. Asking for one thousand pounds would most certainly be viewed as exploitation of the poor unless the idea of saving the world was held to be a genuine goal. It was. A world war demanded sacrifice and support, including financial support. In a discussion of the everyday work of The Salvation Army in 1902, it was written:

> No parish or parochial views of an Officer's life are allowed to rule; in fact, he is trained from his spiritual infancy to understand John Wesley's charter—"The World is my Parish." Not as a sentiment, but as a principle which must find fitting expression in gifts of flesh and blood, and gold and silver.[15]

Those who would be officers (ordained clergy) in this Army of Salvation were impressed with this worldwide calling. In the 1893 issue of *The Officer*, Booth warned: "Is there not a danger of our becoming, as officers, too *national*, and forgetting that the *world* is our God-appointed parish?"[16] In "The Call of the Past to the Present" Booth wrote:

> ... for one thing, THE ARMY MANIFESTED A WORLD-SPIRIT. ... It has been possessed by the grand idea that something was commenced on the hill of Calvary, ... which concerned every branch of the human race; nay every individual of the human family.[17]

Bramwell Booth, speaking to cadets at the International Training College in London, informed them: "You do not fully realise it at present, but you are beginning to realise it—that more and more The Army will show the world the great truth that Jesus Christ died for all."[18]

To many, the idea of a "Salvation Army" and its worldwide mission was pompous to say the least. One writer, known only by his initials, charged:

> A man of God could no more pretend to set up the kingdom of God in the spirit which pervades your public works, as the 'General of the Salvation Army,' than he could give way to the most loathsome and wicked deeds of the flesh.[19]

The self-confidence of the early salvationists was often

viewed with distain. One critic wrote:

> Referring to their recent Congress held at the opening of
> their new hall at Clapton, the *War Cry* says:—'That Congress
> of Clapton will never cease to produce its fruits whilst men
> live on earth. We have been with God for a week, and the
> nation has looked on. Even our enemies are forced to confess
> that our faces shine, and they will find out a great deal more
> by-and-by.' One cannot help contrasting the case of Moses
> who 'wist not that his face shone,' with the self-confidence
> expressed in the above extract.[20]

One of the best known and most respected critics of the
early Army and its General was T. H. Huxley. He saw in the
Army a despotism undergirded by a dangerous fanaticism.
Huxley declared:

> Few social evils are of greater magnitude than uninstructed
> and unchastened religious fanaticism; no personal habit more
> surely degrades the conscience and the intellect than blind
> and unhesitating obedience to unlimited authority.[21]

Inglis, commenting on Huxley's position, asserted that his letters to *The Times,* written to discourage support for the Army

> ... were an attack less on the social theory of Booth's book
> than on the religious system of its author. Harlotry, intemper-
> ance and even starvation seemed to Huxley lesser evils than
> that 'the intellect of a nation' should be 'put down by orga-
> nized fanaticism', and that political and industrial affairs
> should be at the mercy of a despot whose chief thought was to
> make his fanaticism prevail.[22]

Describing the Army and Booth as a new papacy, another
charged:

> ... an organisation ... has been developed into a sect of the
> most exclusive and rigorous description, governed by a mili-
> tary despotism, the supreme and entire control of which is
> placed in the hands of its chief officer, who makes its laws,
> promulgates its creeds, defines its dogmas, and enunciates its
> faith, and that too without any advisory council, and against
> whose will and fiat there is no possible appeal.[23]

This criticism was stirred up not by what the Army was

doing or writing, but by what it essentially was. It was a living organism that caught people's imaginations for ill as well as good. Its dramatic nature gave rise to all kinds of mental images about what it might be and what it might become. One of the most sensational criticisms was a piece of fiction written as a prophecy of what the Army would be in the twentieth century. It appeared in 1890, titled, *Pope Booth, The Salvation Army, A.D. 1950.*

> 'Shattered twenty years ago, now only existing here and there in fragments and in secret. So with all forms of faith but that originated by the Prophet Booth.'
>
> 'The *Prophet* Booth?'
>
> 'Yes; so he is now called although *he* laid no claim to the title. Stead, sixty years ago, declared him to be on a level with the Prophets, and pronounced his Army to be the greatest movement in the religious world since the time of the Apostles. So it was, perhaps, in the first Booth's time, but those who came after him have grown like unto the old Popes of Rome. The lust of temporal power has laid hold of them.'[24]

The writer caught the idea of a religious army, and even gave it the benefit of the doubt that it might be an army of God. He recognized the power potential of this Army for ill. The Army, from Booth down to the rank-and-file also understood this power, but had greater optimism that the Army would continue to be a power for God and good.

Undergirding the notion of an Army of God engaged in world conquest, was the absolute conviction that the Army had been divinely called into being. This sense of divine origin was with Booth's work from the beginning of the Christian Mission. The mission magazine declared: ". . . in answer to prayer, He has sent us forth repeatedly to break the long, wearly spell of night, and organise light and life such as only Divine power can originate."[25]

> Others, thank God! have been raised up to do somewhat similar work, which we would not for a moment undervalue;

but if we are blamed for thinking that the Lord has created and prospered this Mission to do a special and a glorious work amongst the masses of our countrymen, we would point to the history of our FIRST YEAR IN MIDDLESBRO' as an abundant justification.[26]

In the same magazine, George Railton again wrote:

Oh, how the very thought of the mighty burden lying at our door overcomes us! How can we go on writing about it, or talking about it? We must be off to hold up Jesus Christ before these hundred cities in one. God help us to be faithful to our mighty calling![27]

A group of churchmen interviewing Booth reported: "He looked on the movement as having a definite origination and a definite sustenation. He believed it was God who was doing it, and moving up and down the land."[28] In Waller's assessment of the Army in 1882, he wrote:

Now what is the conclusion to which these reflections guide us, but this?—that this movement of the Salvation Army is from the Lord. He is evidently lifting up a standard against the unbelief and wickedness which are in the world.[29]

It is well for us, my dear brethren, to ponder these things in all humility and fear. Such stirrings in the depths of society do not come of man's unaided power. Be assured that the Spirit of the Lord is working mightily amongst us, and may He bless every earnest endeavour to glorify His name.[30]

George Railton stated simply: "The Army has been a great success, of course, simply because God has made and let and sustained it."[31] The clarity of the Army's conviction to all concerned was illustrated by La Comtesse Agenor de Gasparin who wrote sarcastically:

The Army is *the Army of God*. The orders of the chief are *the orders of God*. To be converted to the Army is to be *converted to God*. To give yourself to the Army is to be *saved by God*. To give up all for the Army is to *give up all for God*.[32]

In an unpublished address to cadets, Bramwell Booth asserted: ". . . you must believe that the Army is raised up by God

—you must believe that or it is useless for you to come to this place—you must believe that He has His hand on the arrangements. . . ."[33] Bramwell,. speaking about Commissioner Railton, his father's first lieutenant and the first commissioner of The Salvation Army, noted:

> Even in the occasional differences which he had with his leaders on matters of more or less importance, and some of them were really important, his absolute confidence in the Divine origin of the work and in the ultimate Divine guidance of its administrators ever brought him through into calmer waters.[34]

In the first issue of *The Salvationist*, the magazine of the newly formed Salvation Army, a letter signed by a company of community notables was included. In that letter they asserted:

> Whilst we cannot mark with our approval every bill issued, every expression used, and every measure employed by this "Salvation Army," we feel that the great spiritual results achieved, stamp the work as being of God and not of man, and therefore one which ought to be helped rather than criticised.[35]

Bairstow wrote:

> It is useless to deny that God has been with these people and noble leaders, for in the midst of their innumerable persecutions, slanders, and even death itself, they have sought to win the world from sin and misery, and in a great measure they have succeeded. God has vouchsafed a large outpouring of His Spirit upon them, and they have been led by the Spirit. Still, man's part in the work of saving the lost has been more than ever before brought to the fore.[36]

A salvationist declared:

> If God bases any hopes on anyone for the salvation of the world it must be on The Salvation Army. If we are unfaithful, God will take away our candlestick out of its place. There are quite enough lifeless organisations in the world without our adding one more.[37]

What was experienced as a sense of divine origin within the movement of The Salvation Army became a sense of divine calling within the individual lives of its members. Salvationists believed that God was calling them apart for this special ministry and expression. This sense of divine calling was initiated and enhanced by the early leaders of the movement, especially the founder.

There was no question in Booth's mind or in the minds of friends and foes alike that he believed himself called of God to lead this peculiar movement. In a pamphlet of 1884, Albert Musprat, assessing the value of The Salvation Army to religion, records this conclusion regarding Booth's understanding of his own position.

> Mr. Booth was not chosen by the multitude as were the seven deacons (*Acts vi*), for it is contrary to his doctrine. Mrs. Booth says, 'God made him a general.' And Mr. Booth himself says, 'No man taketh this honour unto himself, but he that is called of God, as Aaron was appointed to the priesthood' (page 12 *Critics of the Salvation Army*).[38]

In times of social and moral upheavel, great leaders are sought who will lead the people out of bondage and confusion and their own waywardness. In England, the later years of the nineteenth century were just such times. In *Christianity and the Working Classes* this need was given literal expression.

> It may be there will rise up again a great Christian teacher whose message the working people again will hear gladly; maybe he will gather them about him into a new Christian fellowship. Such a man would seem to need more of the spirit of Francis of Assisi than of Wesley, since his first essential would have to be 'the inestimable treasure of most holy poverty.' Wesley's was the voice of the middle classes. This one's will be the voice of the working classes.[39]

Booth was such a voice, but his sense of divine calling and the authority he commanded went beyond that of a great teacher.

Booth's unique sense of calling was cast in the mold of the prophets of old. In his article regarding "First Principles," he asserted: "'I am your leader.'"[40] "'. . . I will stick to my post till God discharges me.'"[41] Inglis reported that Catherine urged her husband to work outside the Church where he would be free to follow God's leading. He commented:

> Booth needed little persuading, so overwhelmed was he by a sense of the urgency of saving the heathen masses, so disappointed by the lethargy of the churches and by the antipathy he had aroused in them, and so serenely confident that the hand of the Lord was upon him.[42]

This sense of divine presence was experienced in the most prophetically intimate terms.

> A voice seemed to be eversounding in my ears, 'Why go to Derby, or anywhere else, to find souls who need the gospel? Here they are; tens and hundreds of thousands, at your very door. Preach to them the unsearchable riches of Christ. I will help you - your need shall be supplied.'[43]

Booth ever saw himself as a spokesman of God. He announced to his officers: "Under God, I have been the means of calling you out and sending you[r] forth on this great mission."[44] He prayed for and he believed that he received God's guidance in all of his plans for the work of the Army. In his article on "First Principles" he wrote:

> 'The time has surely come when I can speak to you with authority and expect you to follow me, even though you may not understand everything. I do not ask you to go *against* your reason, but I may ask you to go *above* and *beyond* it.'[45]

"'Now I do want a continuation of your confidence, for I feel God has been wonderfully enlightening my intelligence of late.'"[46] It was through the organ of *The Officer* that Booth sought to give prophetical guidance to his, now, worldwide Army. He proposed to

> . . .unfold the plans of action which God and His Providence may be pleased to give me, utter such warnings as

appear needful, from time to time. . .to tell you all that is in my heart concerning this warfare with the world, the flesh, and the devil, which you ought to know.[47]

Booth's most famous book, *In Darkest England and the Way Out,* was considered by him to be God's given plans through God's own spokesman.

> That my name is mixed up with the enterprise is an acci-
> dent. I take no personal credit. The book is the outcome of the
> circumstances in which my public life has been cradled. God
> drove me into the 'Dark Forest' years ago, and has been lead-
> ing me to and fro in that wilderness ever since. He has shown
> me everything that I have described, and put into my heart
> the plans that I have proposed. I am His servant. I do His bid-
> ding. Nay, I verily believe I have been His mouthpiece in all I
> have said in this volume.[48]

Of Booth and his work, Heathcote remarked:

> If good deeds and good intentions are of any value at all,
> then surely we have had a prophet amongst us; and if we
> have failed to recognise him as such, generations to come will
> condemn us when they honour the name of William Booth,
> the first General of the Salvation Army.[49]

Without doubt Booth's prophetical posture and burning passion for God's work of redemption was the single most dynamic force in establishing the work and the ethos of the early Army. Together with a prophet's heart of zeal and compassion, Booth expected all who would work with him to recognize a prophetical authority in his word. In his thoughts on leadership, he wrote:

> He will inspire them so that they will feel no disposition
> to argue. You know how this spirit is going out of this
> world. Men now will know the reason for everything. True
> Leadership is passing away, or only expressing itself in the
> Radical gabble of the Democratic rabble. The influence of
> the true Leader is the reverse of the spirit of the age. When
> he speaks the people believe him and go to fulfill his com-
> mands and more or less worship him, but it is based on the
> love of him.[50]

Asked about his one-man rule, Booth's answer was:

> . . .the reason is as novel as the situation is old: 'I have been
> sent into the world,' says Mr. Booth to his questioner, 'to do
> the Lord's gutter work. Bitter experience has taught me that
> nothing less than the strong hand of absolute power held over
> them will keep many of my evangelists from getting too fine
> for this work. They begin to get respectable, and to turn their
> noses at the gutter, out of which I have lifted them.'[51]

Other Army leaders were recognized as prophet types.
Bramwell considered John Lawley as one such individual.
He reported Lawley's call to be an evangelist in dramatical-
ly prophetical terms.

> 'Mother, I see it more clearly than before: I should offer myself to
> be an evangelist,'
> In silence, for some moments, the little woman surveyed
> her son, radiant with holy enthusiasm, then, once and for all,
> she laid her Isaac on the altar, and replied in her gentle, cooing
> voice, 'Then Johnny, if you must go, you shall go. The Lord
> will provide.'[52]

Bramwell went on to assert that to the reality and love of
Jesus in Lawley's heart ". . . was added the soul of a mystic
and the eyes and message of a prophet."[53]

> Where many men discerned no star in the sky, Lawley saw
> a clear light shining; where others might sniff a suggestion of
> smoke, Lawley saw Hell uncovered, with all the horrors of the
> abode of the lost. As for Heaven, he saw right into it; he sang
> about it, and wrote about it until he made others think of it,
> believe in it, choose it, and live for it.[54]

Some saw prophetic qualities in the rank and file as well
as the leaders of the Army. A letter to the editor of the
Consett Guardian speaks of the leader of a Salvation Army
meeting.

> 'Their leader seemed to be greatly favoured by the earnest
> appeal of love she was constrained to deliver to the audience,
> for she spoke with authority, and not as a scribe. I may go fur-
> ther—that is, more like the mouthpiece of the unctions of the
> Divine spirit, for the power of God was over all.'[55]

Other characteristics of the Army's expression were being recognized as prophetic in nature. In an article appearing in The *Daily News*, the Army's ministry is described as prophetic because of the passionate nature of its work.

> "Every diligent reader of the New Testament ought to suspect, what every reader of early Church history knows, how essential was the part played by the prophetic ministry, which was a passionate outpouring of the heart.[56]

> The Salvation Army has been guilty of many extravagances, repulsive, no doubt, to fastidious persons, but within these extravagances, real or so-called, there throbbed a heart of sympathy, while an instinct of practical good sense guided it to achievements which were the surest proof of its wisdom, and the amplest vindication of the divinity of its mission.[57]

The opposition generated by the Army's novel and sensational methods was regarded by early Army leaders as a natural reaction of the world to the prophets. Railton wrote:

> Only in this spirit of utter disregard for public opinion have God's prophets, in all ages been able to do their work, and only whilst they remain indifferent to men's scorn and opposition, can the Soldiers of The Salvation Army properly discharge their task of 'warning and teaching every man,' in all wisdom.[58]

The courage to do the new, even questionable, was identified as prophetical action. Reporting on a lecture delivered by Mrs. Booth in St. James Hall, *The Times* reported:

> Their principle was that of adaptation of means to end. As the prophets under the command of God had done things strange in the sight of the Jews to arouse them to a sense of their iniquity, so they now tried by striking and novel appeals to arouse the attention of the unthinking, untaught, and unwashed, whom all other efforts had failed to reach. Christ had chosen men of the people to preach his Word, and the workers in this mission were men and women of the people sent to carry the Gospel to the people.[59]

There was one characteristic of the prophetical nature of Booth and his movement that carried the notion of the movement beyond that of an Army of God. Booth's son

Herbert isolates this characteristic although he does not use the term prophetical or any of its derivatives.

'Now how often, dear General, we have all heard you say that the government of the Army was in its nature more paternal than military? How often you have reminded us that this spirit was its soul guarantee of permanence.'[60]

'When the Army grew, the family spirit and method grew with it. In the early days you were as a father in the midst of your people. You are regarded as such today. The movement will never know the full power of the spell of your personal influence until you are gone.'[61]

What Herbert did not say regarding the personal influence of his father, a writer in *The Primitive Methodist Review* had said.

General Booth's power of organisation and his influence over men have enabled him to consolidate and keep together forces that would have gone to pieces under the rule of a lesser genius; but does not this praise carry with it a necessary condemnation—for does it not suggest how a difficulty might arise whenever the General might pass away? We hope this day may be long distant, and that, occur when it may, Elijah's mantel may drop on Elisha's shoulders.[62]

The paternal spirit of Booth the Founder was much more a prophetic than a military characteristic. Booth was no war lord. He was a spokesman of God. As Herbert declared, this paternal spirit brought to the movement a familial ethos whereby Booth's following understood themselves to be a new people of God. Wyndham Heathcote, one-time officer, quoted from the "Field Secretary's Notes" regarding the Army's understanding of itself.

History repeats itself! Nonsense! History does not repeat itself! When will people understand that we are not a revival of the Quakers or the Primitive Methodists? Cannot God make a new thing on the earth?[63]

To a Salvationist, the birth of the Army in Whitechapel appeared to be a renewal of Pentecost. It was a genuine outburst of spiritual enthusiasm. It was as though Christianity was thrown into its first simplicity and zeal into the heart of the crowded metropolis, to shape and form itself once more.[64]

Heathcote argued: "It must be obvious that the Army owes a great deal, and even the possibility of its existence, to the previous existence of other bodies."[65] The Army did not deny that it had been influenced in many ways and from many areas. What it understood was that whatever the influences, something new had come into being under the inspiration of God himself. This notion found dramatic expression in *The Officer* of 1893 in an article on the work of officers. "Our work . . . to create a *new* people for God out of the raw material around us."[66] Like Ezekiel our Army is to come ". . . from the dead."[67] ". . . dead in sin, dead to their highest interests, dead to God's claims, dead to the dangers of eternity without God; . . ."[68] "To definitely get a sinner converted and enrolled and in fighting form, is a greater victory than putting a dozen people on the rolls, who are members of churches and missions, . . ."[69] "*Go for the dead,* and out of those ranks create a force who shall stand for God."[70] "Nothing calls attention in the house so much as the new baby."[71]

Bryan Wilson asserts that in the later years of Booth's Generalship there was a tendency to deify the Army.[72] He further asserts that this tendency was exploited by Bramwell who lacked his father's charisma. The implication is that the prophetical sense inherent in Booth and other early leaders of the Army as well as the notion of a peculiar people of God did not continue in strength past the Army's formative years. Inglis agreed with this claim. He wrote:

> Despite Booth's declaration that he would never let his Army become one more sect, that was its destiny. What had once been sensational in its methods, preserved in the next generation, became old-fashioned. Henceforth it was to be run not by prophets but by administrators, and its ways became rather less different than those of other sects. Peculiarities remained. Its officers moved more easily than most ordained ministers through slums and into public houses, and they

gained a reputation for dispensing social relief with a lack of condescension or inquisition . . . .[73]

That a case might be made for a transition from prophetical authority to administrative decision, supports the contention that the early Army possessed this sense of prophetical presence in the midst of a notion of a peculiar people of God.

The dramatic nature of these notions is well illustrated in Bramwell Booth's quote of Johnston Ross and his answer to the statement of Ross.

'. . . If by your scholarship you so make to live again the classic scenes in which the Nazarene moved and taught, that I am made conscious of the long centuries that divide Him from me; then all the more if you would secure the abiding of my faith in Him, you must let me see how He can still reach *me*, and stand for *me*. How the wings of His gracious personality can be outstretched to cover *me*.'

It is because we of The Salvation Army so see how that can be, nay, see daily and hourly as the hands move round the dial of the clock, that those wings are outstretched to cover the most needy, that the progress of our work continues to be one of the great spiritual facts of the world's history.[74]

It is fitting that the conclusion of this chapter is aptly introduced by the words of one of the earliest of Army leaders, and one closest to William Booth in those formative days. Commissioner Railton, in writing the biography of William Booth, asserted: ". . . the whole theory of a Divine Army and of War, must remain forever one of the strongest features of his life's work."[75] It should be added that the most powerful notion, and that to which all of the drama of the Army's theological constructs and expression led was this notion of a new people.

But you are a chosen people, a royal priesthood, a holy nation, a people belonging to God, that you may declare the praises of him who called you out of darkness into his wonderful light. Once you were not a people, but now you are the people of God; once you had not received mercy, but now you have received mercy. [I Peter 2:9-10, NIV]

Chapter XIV
Conclusion

There were many adjectives that were appropriate descriptions of The Salvation Army in its formative years, such as zealous, committed, involved, called, burdened, and loving, to mention but a few. These characteristics were brought into the service of a declared sense of prophetic vision. This was not a vision expressed in foretelling or forecasting. It was a vision comprised of theological ideas, dramatic in nature, centering upon the conquest of the world by God's righteousness, holiness, and love.

This endeavor at conquest was nothing less than a crusade of salvation with the world as the battlefield and the world of individuals as the lost needing to be saved. From its inception as a mission, and then the Army, the theology of salvation embraced a multitude of concerns.

Inherent in this theology of salvation, especially so because of the class of people for which the Army felt a peculiar burden, was a serious and extensive social concern. From the beginning, the Army believed that social conditions had a direct bearing on the attitude with which the poor and needy considered Christianity. Early Salvationists were convinced that people could not seriously contemplate their soul's salvation when their physical survival itself was in question. Before long, the expressions of this social concern within the Army became so powerful that even with the irreverence and sensationalism attached to the Army's religious expression, more and more people came to accept and later admire the Army because of what it was doing for the poor and destitute, as well as the spirit of love and selflessness with which that work was carried forward.

This serious, social consciousness was expressed in hundreds of social services about which many people have written. These services have been by far the most publicized aspects of The Salvation Army. In the United States, where the Army has labored officially since 1880, most of the population is totally unaware that the Army is a legally constituted denomination of the Christian faith. Even in England where the Army began, while the religious nature of the Army is more familiar to the general public, it is still the Army's work with the down-and-outer that is the most recognized.

There were occasions when the Army confronted social evils directly. The Army's most extensive program of social concern was, of course, Booth's "Darkest England" scheme, which has been discussed. The Army also directly confronted social evils in such places as the match industry, resulting in legislation that prohibited the use of poisonous substances harmful to the workers and in juvenile vice, where laws were passed to raise the age of consent for young girls. However, these more isolated cases of Army action against social institutions should not be misconstrued to imply a developed concept of social sin whereby the Army considered as a methodology the direct opposition of social institutions which might be considered sinful, as for example the alcohol or tobacco industries.

The early Army concentrated on conducting its affairs with a high degree of Christian integrity and genuine love to provide a powerful contrast to any expression of life emphasizing worldliness and contributing to the sinfulness of the people. However, the Army held firmly to the position that the only way to bring the salvation of Christ into prominence among the people of the earth was through personal evangelism.

The Army concentrated on those ministries and services that gave its officers and soldiers the best opportunities to come into a one-to-one relationship with the people they were trying to save. Person-to-person evangelism, often made possible through the expression of social concern, was the recognized method for the Army's worldwide, salvation mission. To those within the Army movement, social work was always considered to be a means to an end, even though recognized as an appropriate obligation of Christian expression. The salvation of the individual soul was the primary goal toward which all work was focused. A theology of salvation, both in its individual sense of personal religious experience and in its corporate sense as a mission to a world lost in sin, was the precipitating and preeminent feature of this movement. To consider the essence of The Salvation Army in terms of any other emphasis is to misunderstand the Army.

This theology of salvation was never limited to a narrow view of sins forgiven, or, in more technical terms, justification and regeneration. For The Salvation Army, salvation was the whole of life, it was a way to live. It was only natural that the doctrine of sanctification, which was deep, pervasive, spiritual cleansing, should be regarded as the desired development of the salvation experience. This relationship between sanctification and salvation became doubly important in light of the Army's sense of worldwide mission, which required the power of the sanctified life.

The question of whether a person could get to heaven if he were only saved and not sanctified was little entertained by the Army. It is undeniable that the Army believed that faith in Christ alone, with its necessary conditions of contrition and repentance, was enough to gain forgiveness of sins making one eligible for heaven. However, this was not a point of doctrine upon which to dwell. This was a minimal condition of faith, a beginning faith and only a beginning. The Army was living in the midst of a church community it considered to be cold, mediocre, and ineffective in reaching the millions alienated from its sanctuaries. It was imperative that new converts get beyond the basics to the more demanding and far-reaching ramifications of the salvation experience. For the Army convert, the importance of one's personal salvation was easily and necessarily transformed into a burden for the world of lost sinners, which in turn necessitated a cleansed and pure nature so that divine power for this mission might be imparted.

In a society governed by a dominant word culture, there was little sympathy for the poor who were related more to the image culture of a past day. Exploited and alienated, these lower classes found themselves disfranchised in situation and aspiration. The Army's theological constructs emphasized the power and purpose of salvation. This message held out a welcome to the masses to come into the family of God. They could belong. They were offered a home.

While Booth vehemently declared never to allow his Army to become just another church sect, Inglis is correct in arguing that this was the Army's destiny. In light of this transition certain concerns arise in terms of this early salvation theology.

It was not Army methodology that made possible the close, almost immediate relationship between salvation and sanctification. The possibility existed because the Army was essentially a movement. As a movement of salvation, its goals and purposes were relatively few and specific. To oversimplify, a movement gives the impression that it has one thing to do. People join this movement to accomplish this goal. If a person is not interested in the goal, he does not join the movement.

In the formative years of the Army, people joined the movement to win the world for Christ. They accepted a standard of holiness as a requisite for this great mission. People who came to the Army were quickly made aware that a full surrender to God was necessary, first so that their sins might be forgiven and then so that God could use them as channels of blessing. However, as the second, third, and fourth generations of Salvationists have come along, the primary goal of the Army, while still direct and clear, for many people is not the motivating principle as they seek membership. As children are born into the ranks of The Salvation Army, they no longer attend because they identify with its mission. They attend because their parents bring them. As they grow up in the Army, they are not automatically at the point of full surrender or even seriously considering it. They need to be taught about their sins and carnality. They need to be taught to think about others before themselves.

This is one sense in which a movement is transformed into a church. The nature of the Church is to work with its own people, teaching them, inspiring them, chastening them, all in an effort to help them mature to the point where, to them, the mission of the Church is once again the contemplative, emotional, and deeply sober rallying point of the movement. The movement must never be abandoned, even within the concept of the Church, while the Church must ever be more than the movement.

I believe that it is this problem of transition with which the Army is grappling today. Its concerns as a movement have outweighed its concerns as a Church, and now it has some catching up to do. It must engage in the process of instructional programs that teach the Army, and especially its theology, as catechism classes of a church do. It must also recognize the continual need of man's emotional nature and the value of observances that edify and intensify the spiritual life of its people as sacramental systems are inclined to do.

It might be argued that these aids have never been successful in the Church. The Church, with all of its teachings and ritualistic accoutrements, is still relatively ineffectual, mediocre, and apathetic. However, the laws and liturgy given to the Israelites of old by God himself resulted in some miserable failures. Most would be quite hesitant to lay the blame for this before the laws and the liturgy rather than the people. The same holds true for today. The Church with its many facets is not the problem. However, a dramatic theology is never outdated and just as necessary today. This study does present a viable model for churches to consider.

In The Salvation Army's early years, this dramatic theology stirred the imagination with all kinds of possibilities. At the same time, it rested on a firm basis of theological orthodoxy. In the wedding of these two attributes the foundation of a dynamic and innovative expression of nineteenth-century evangelicalism was laid. It was this theology around which the programs and goals of The Salvation Army were organized. It was also this theology that was the single most important feature in attracting the Army's membership and establishing it as a religious and charitable organization with a worldwide expression. Through the dramatic expression of this theology, which presented doctrinal positions in highly visual and pictorial images compatible with the cultural characteristics of the poor, not only were the poor encouraged to become part of this family of God; even more, they were offered a hope for the future. They found not only a home but also a new way of life with values and aspirations for the present and for eternity.

Dramatic expression in the Church is always necessary. People living at the cutting edge of life and death, as well as those more comfortable and secure, must be made to appreciate, and to be deeply moved by, the realities of eternal reward and punishment. Only through dramatic expression, where dramatic language has a one-to-one correspondence with dramatic living, will the truth of this theology of salvation have an opportunity to be discovered and desired. When a highly pictorial, image-oriented, sensational language is embodied by human flesh, language becomes much more than rhetoric. Language gains genuine life and true drama. In this real union, letter and spirit meet and become one. It becomes possible for death, which is always a danger in the letter, and fanaticism, which is always a danger in the spirit, to be avoided and authentic life realized.

Finally, in the study of the theology of The Salvation Army in its formative years, we are confronted with a progressive or evolutionary notion. It can be understood in terms of beginning, becoming, and being. In Part I the soil necessary for the beginning of a new religious movement is uncovered. In Part II, people are confronted with the subject matter of this new movement which, in itself, is an invitation to become part of this new religious order. In Part III, this religious order, expressed in novel form, becomes something other than what it was initially.

In The Salvation Army, somewhat in the sense of the Hegelian dialectic, through theses, antitheses, and syntheses, an organism was formed which contained characteristics of previous organisms and yet was totally new. The foundation of a church laid in Part II through the doctrines of salvation, sanctification, and the relationship of God and man as understood by the Army, resulted in something other than a church and even an Army. In Part III the notion of an Army along with its dramatic expression carried the idea of community to a visionary notion of a new people of God somewhat on the order of the Israelites of old.

This evolution is still continuing in the Army's transition from a movement alone, to a more traditional expression of the Church, within which the sense of a movement can be contained. It is highly questionable whether this transition could have been avoided as the Army matured. It is even more questionable that the Army should oppose this transition, since it is doubtful that the Army could continue as only a movement. The Army must strive to retain and develop both its character as a movement and a church, if it is to fulfill its destiny.

In the formative years of the Army, it was the dynamic theology of salvation which resulted in the concept of a new people of God and endowed the movement with growing as well as staying power. The Army truly became an expression of its theology. Unless this theology is again raised to preeminence in the hearts, minds, and lives of the Army's people today, The Salvation Army will be left with a mission that defies its spiritual capabilities. This theology of salvation can only be lifted up as the Army develops the strengths and mysteries of the Church, even if in a peculiarly Army way, as well as the commitment and urgency of the movement.

Notes and References

Chapter II

1. Harold Begbie, Life of *William Booth: The Founder of The Salvation Army*, (London: Macmillan & Co., St. Martin's Street), I, 15.

2. Ibid., pp. 24-25.

3. Ibid., pp. 29-30.

4. Robert Sandall, *The History of The Salvation Army*, (London: Thomas Nelson and Sons Ltd, 1947), I, 3.

5. St. John Ervine, *God's Soldier: General William Booth*, (New York: Macmillan Company, 1935), I, 34.

6. Ibid.

7. Sandall, *Hist. of Sal. Army*, I, 4.

8. Ervine, *God's Soldier*, I, 36-37.

9. Catherine Bramwell-Booth, *Catherine Booth* (London: Hodder and Stoughton, 1973), p. 18.

10. Ibid., pp. 18-19.

11. Ibid., p. 22.

12. Ibid., p. 29.

13. Ibid.

14. Ibid.

15. Ibid., p. 33.

16. Ibid., p. 34.

17. Ibid., p. 44.

18. Sandall, *Hist. of Sal. Army*, I, 5-11.

19. Ibid., pp. 13-16.

20. Ibid., p. 68.

21. Ibid., p. 198.

22. Ibid., p. 207.

23. Ibid., p. 236.

24. Ibid., p. 237.

25. Ibid., p. 234.

26. Robert Sandall, *The History of The Salvation Army*, (London: Thomas Nelson, 1950), II, 24.

27. Ibid., p. 65.

28. Ibid., p. 232.

29. Ibid., p. 17.

30. Ibid., p. 299.

31. Ibid., p. 300.

32. Arch R. Wiggins, *The History of The Salvation Army*, (London: Thomas Nelson, 1964), IV, 3-107.

33. Sandall, *Hist. of Sal. Army*, II, 33.

34. Ibid., p. 34.

35. Ibid., p. 33.

36. Ibid., p. 34.

37. Ibid., p. 50.

38. Ibid., p. 38.

39. Ibid., p. 131.

40. Ibid.

41. Ibid., p. 126.

Chapter III

1. W. Salt, *A Memorial of The Wesleyan Methodist New Connexion: Containing A Short Account of the Circuit Preachers Who Have Died; and A General Statement of the Leading Transactions of the Connexion From Its Formations in 1797 to the Present Time* (Nottingham: Printed and sold by Sutton and Son, 1823), p. 252.

2. Ibid., p. 121.

3. Ibid., pp. 122-23.

4. Mr. Allin and others, *The Jubilee of the Methodist New Connexion: Being A Grateful Memorial of the Origin, Government, and History of the Denomination* (London: John Bakewell, 80, Newgate Street, 1848), 140-41.

5. Ibid., p. 54.

6. Salt, *Memorial of . . . Meth. New Connexion*, p. 138.

7. Ibid., p. 254.

8. Ibid., p. 221.

9. Ibid.

10. Ibid., pp. 153-54; for S.A. doctrines see also *The Songbook of The Salvation Army* (New York: The Salvation Army Supplies, Printing and Publishing Department, 1960), p. 373; R.S. doctrines were found on a Xerox copy, *War Cry*, July 6, 1940.

11. Rev. Allen Rees, *Methodism and The Salvation Army: A Paper Read Before the London Wesleyan Preachers' Meeting, On Monday, December 19th, 1881* (Hayman Brothers and Lilly, 1881), p. 4.

Chapter IV

1. Frederick Copleston, *A History of Philosophy*, Vol. VIII: *Modern Philosophy*, Part I, *British Empiricism and the Idealist Movement in Great Britain* (Garden City, New York: Image Books, 1967), p. 26.

2. Ibid., pp. 38-40.

3. David Thomson, *England in the Nineteenth Century*, 1815-1914 (Viking Penguin Inc., 1950), pp. 45-46.

4. Kathleen Heasman, *Evangelicals in Action: An Appraisal of Their Social Work in the Victorian Era* (London: Geoffrey Bles, 1962), p. 6.

5. Ibid.

6. Owen Chadwick, *The Victorian Church*, I: Part I (3d ed.; London: Adam & Charles Black, 1971), 5.

7. Hugh McLeod, *Class and Religion in the Late Victorian City* (London: Croom Helm Ltd, 1974), p. 217.

8. Ibid.

9. Ibid., p. 222.

10. Chadwick, *The Vic. Chr.*, p. 527.

11. McLeod, *Class and Religion*, p. 13.

12. Ibid., p. 24.

13. Ibid., p. 14.

14. Ibid., p. 152.

15. Ibid., p. 13.

16. Ibid., p. 199.

17. Ibid., p. 151.

18. Ibid., pp. 151-52.

19. Ibid., pp. 154-55.

20. Ibid., p. 156.

21. Ibid., p. 148.

22. Ibid., p. 147.

23. Ibid., p. 143.

24. Ibid., p. 144.

25. Ibid., p. 43.

26. Ibid., p. 282.

27. Ibid., p. 69.

28. George S. Railton, *General Booth* (2d ed.; London: Hodder and Stoughton, 1912), p. 8.

29. Ibid., p. 9.

30. Prebendary Wilson Carlile, "The Church Army," *Modern Evangelistic Movements*, ed. Two University Men (London: Thomson & Cowan, 1924), p. 22.

31. Ibid., p. 21.

32. Ibid., p. 36.

33. "The Bishop of Melbourne on The Salvation Army," *All The World*, I, 3(January, 1885), 35.

34. Mrs. Booth, "Our Commission," *All The World*, I, 6(April, 1885), 84.

Chapter VI

1. William Booth, "Our New Name," *The Salvationist With Which Is Incorporated the Christian Mission Magazine, Being The Organ of The Salvation Army*, XI, 1(January, 1879), 1.

2. Ibid.

3. William Booth, "The East London Christian Mission," *The East London Evangelist: A Record of Christian Work Among the People, and Organ of the East London Christian Mission*, I (October,1868), 3.

4. Kathleen Heasman, *Evangelicals in Action: An Appraisal of Their Social Work in the Victorian Era* (London: Geoffrey Bles, 1962), p. 14.

5. Catherine Booth, "Conscience," *The Christian Mission Magazine*, IX (January, 1877), 5.

6. *The Doctrines of The Salvation Army* (London: Salvationist Publishing and Supplies, Ltd., 1881), p. 17.

7. *The Darkest England Gazette: The Official Newspaper of the Social Operations of The Salvation Army* (London), July 15, 1893, p. 7.

8. Ibid.

9. George Haw (ed.), *Christianity and the Working Classes* (London: Macmillan & Co., 1906), p. 160.

10. G. S. Railton, "Up," *The Christian Mission Magazine*, VIII (May, 1876), 99.

11. Ibid.

12. William Booth, "How to Manage A Mission Station," *The Christian Mission Magazine*, VIII (September, 1876), 151.

13. William Booth, "Christian Mission Work, The Month," *The Christian Mission Magazine*, VIII (September, 1876), 212.

14. "Fight," *All The World*, I, 7(May, 1885), 111.

15. Ibid., p. 112.

16. "Go," *All The World*, I, 1(November, 1884), 2-3.

17. Commissioner Booth Tucker, "Editor's Chat," *The Officer*, I, 2(February, 1893), 48.

18. Colonel Lawley, "The 'Jubilee Thousand' Candidates," *The Officer*, II, 6(June, 1894), 168.

19. *Doctrines of S.A.*, p. 47.

20. Rev. Wyndham S. Heathcote, *My Salvation Army Experience* (London: Marshall Brothers, 10, Paternoster Row, E.C., 1891), p. 13

21. "Go in the Power of the Holy Ghost," *All The World*, I, 2(December, 1884), 13.

22. "Go," *All The World*, p. 1.

23. Ibid., p. 4.

24. "No Retreat," *All The World*, I, 3(December, 1884), 25.

25. *Spiritual Conflict: A Glance at the Every Day Work of The Salvation Army* (London: 101, Queen Victoria Street, E.C., 1902), p. 7.

26. Colonel Lucy Booth, "Burning Questions," *The Officer*, II, 6(June 1894), 177.

27. Mrs. Booth, "The Kingdom of Christ," *All The World*, I, 11(September, 1885), 208-209.

28. George S. Railton, *General Booth* (2d ed.; London: Hodder and Stoughton, 1912), p. 146.

29. Haw, *Christianity and Working*, pp. 33-34.

30. Lawley, "Jubilee Candidates," *The Officer*, p. 168.

31. *Doctrines of S.A.*, pp. 44-45.

32. "The East London Christian Mission," *The East London Evangelist*, I (December, 1868), 36.

33. Minnie L. Carpenter, *Commissioner John Lawley* (London: Salvationist Publishing and Supplies, Ltd., 1924), p. 114.

34. Railton, *General Booth*, p. 35.

35. "The Prayer Meeting - II," *The Officer*, I, 4(April, 1893), 104.

36. Ibid.

37. Ibid.

38. *Sensation or Salvation* (London: Civil Service Printing and Publishing Company, Limited, 8, Salisbury Court, Fleet Street, E.C., 1883), p. 7.

39. "Opportunity and Responsibility," *The Officer*, II, 6(June, 1894), 166.

40. Ibid., "Incidents and Illustrations," p. 188.

41. *Doctrines of S.A.*, p. 113.

42. K. S. Inglis, *Churches and the Working Classes in Victorian England* (London: Routledge & Kegan Paul, 1963), p. 184.

43. Colonel Lucy Booth, "More of God," *The Officer*, II, 6(June 1894), 176.

44. Ibid., p. 177.

45. Inglis, *Churches*, p. 213.

46. The General, "Fight," *All The World*, I, 7(May 1885), 113.

47. General Bramwell Booth, "Addresses" (unpublished addresses, c. 1925), pp. 114-115.

48. *Opinions of Eminent Persons Upon the Work of The Salvation Army at Home and Abroad* (London: International Headquarters, Queen Victoria Street, London, E.C., 1900), pp. 33-34.

49. Charles Owen, "Visiting," *The East London Evangelist*, I (May 1, 1869), 120.

50. The General, "How to Succeed," *The Officer*, II, 4(April, 1894), 97.

51. Ibid., p. 98.

52. *Talks With Officers of The Salvation Army: Being Interviews Reprinted from 'The Officer Magazine* (London: The Salvation Army Book Department, 1921), p. 18.

53. Bramwell Booth (comp.), *Essays and Sketches* (London: International Headquarters, 101, Queen Victoria Street, E.C., n.d.), p. 25.

54. Railton, *General Booth*, p. 37.

55. Ibid.

56. The General, "The Salvation Army," *The Salvationist*, XI (January 2, 1879), 29.

57. *Spiritual Conflict*, p. 5.

58. "The Salvation Army in Geneva," *The Times* [London], February 21, 1883, p. 12.

59. "The Salvation Army in Geneva," *The Times* [London], February 24, 1883, p. 8.

60. G. S. Railton, *Heathen England* (London: International Headquarters, 101, Queen Victoria Street, E.C., 1891), pp. 144-45.

61. Ibid., p. 145.

62. "A Great Mystery," *All The World*, I, 4(February, 1885), 48.

63. Rev. W. H. Rooper, *General Booth and The Salvation Army* (London: Simpkin, Marshall, Hamilton, Kent, & Co., Limited, 1892), p. 13.

64. "California," *All The World*, I, 2(December, 1884), 23.

65. Dr. Oram, "India," *All The World*, I, 1(November, 1884), 6.

66. Railton, *Heathen England*, p. 145.

67. "The Salvation Army," *The Times* [London], February 2, 1883, p. 7.

68. Railton, *General Booth*, p. 54.

69. Ibid.

70. Mrs. Booth, "Our Commission," *All The World*, I, 6(April, 1885), 83.

71. Ibid.

72. Ibid.

73. William Booth, "The Open Air," *The Officer*, I, 1(January, 1893), 19.

74. Mrs. Booth, "The Kingdom of Christ," *All The World*, I, 11(September, 1885), 207.

75. Ibid.

Chapter VII

1. *Doctrines of S.A.*, p. 55

2. Rev. J. A. Wood, *Perfect Love; or Plain Things for Those Who Need Them* (36th ed.; London: The Salvation Army Book-Room, 1902), p. 71.

3. Ibid.

4. "Sanctification," *The Christian Mission Magazine*, VIII (February 1876), 35.

5. "Our Library," *The Officer*, II, 3(March 1894), pp. 83-84.

6. Wood, *Perfect Love*, pp. 13-14.

7. Ibid., p. 14.

8. Ibid., p. 27.

9. Ibid., p. 23.

10. Mrs. Phoebe Palmer, *Entire Devotion to God* (London: Salvationist Publishing and Supplies, Ltd., n.d.), pp. 166-67.

11. "Holiness: Theory and Practise," *The Officer*, II, 3(March, 1894), 69.

12. Ibid.

13. Ibid.

14. Ibid.

15. Wood, *Perfect Love*, p. 22.

16. "Burning Questions," *The Officer*, II, 3(March 1894), 82.

17. "Subject Notes," *The Officer*, I, 3(March 1893), 88.

18. "Sanctification," *The Christian Mission Magazine*, VIII (February 1876), 35.

19. Ibid., p. 36.

20. Palmer, *Entire Devotion*, p. 40.

21. Wood, *Perfect Love*, p. 64.

22. Ibid., p. 75.

23. Ibid.

24. Ibid., pp. 94-95.

25. "An Episcopalian on Perfect Love," *The Christian Mission Magazine*, VIII (July, 1876), 167.

26. Ibid.

27. W. B. "Letter from William Booth to the Brethren and Sisters Labouring for Jesus in Connection with the Dunedin Hall Christian Mission, Edinburgh," *The East London Evangelist*, I (April 1, 1869), 105.

28. Rev. John Fletcher, "Perfect Love," *The East London Evangelist*, I (September, 1869), 179.

29. The General, "A Fair Wind for Salvation," *The Officer*, I, 4(April, 1893), 99.

30. Wood, *Perfect Love*, p. 77.

31. Ibid., p. 62.

32. Palmer, *Entire Devotion*, pp. 176-177.

33. Wood, *Perfect Love*, p. 59.

34. Palmer, *Entire Devotion*, p. 38.

35. Ibid., p. 153.

36. "The Sheffield Council of War," *The Salvationist*, XI (April, 1879), 89.

37. Bramwell Booth "Addresses," p. 167-68.

38. Ibid., pp. 168-169.

39. Wood, *Perfect Love*, p. 14.

40. The General, *Talks with Officers*, p. 19.

41. *Doctrines of S.A.*, p. 86.

42. Ibid., p. 87.

43. Palmer, *Entire Devotion*, p. 43.

44. Bramwell Booth "Addresses," pp. 87-88.

45. Ibid., p. 89.

46. Ibid., pp. 90-91.

47. Ibid., p. 91.

48. Ibid., p. 92.

49. Ibid., p. 93.

50. Wood, *Perfect Love*, p. 11.

51. Palmer, *Entire Devotion*, p. 31.

52. *Doctrines of S.A.*, p. 82.

53. Wood, *Perfect Love*, p. 69.

54. *Doctrines of S.A.*, pp. 84-85.

55. Colonel Nicol, "Burning Questions," *The Officer*, II, 3(March, 1894), 82.

56. Ibid.

57. Wood, *Perfect Love*, p. 87.

58. Palmer, *Entire Devotion*, p. 89.

59. Wood, *Perfect Love*, p. 99.

60. O.W.L.A., *Some Reasons Why I Do Not Sympathise with the Salvation Army* (London: John F. Shaw and Co., 48, Paternoster Row, E.C., 1882), p. 6.

61. "Art. VI. - The Salvation Army," *The Church Quarterly* Review for April 1882, XIV (April 1882), 119.

62. Ibid., pp. 119-120.

63. *Sensation or Salvation*, p. 14.

64. Ibid.

65. Ibid.

66. "Sanctification," *The Christian Mission Magazine*, VIII (February 1876), 35.

67. *Doctrines of S.A.*, p. 68.

68. Ibid., p. 69.

69. Railton, *Heathen England*, p. 31.

70. Ibid., p. 146.

71. The General, "The Millenium," *All The World*, VI, 8(August, 1890), 343.

72. Wood, *Perfect Love*, p. 61.

73. Palmer, *Entire Devotion*, p. 15.

74. Ibid., pp. 20-21.

75. Ibid., p. 156.

76. *Doctrines of S.A.*, p. 66.

77. Ibid., p. 67.

78. "The Salvation Army," *The Times* [London], May 30, 1882, p. 4.

79. Booth, "Letter...to the Brethren and Sisters Labouring...with the Dunedin Hall Christian Mission," p. 104.

80. Ibid., p. 105.

Chapter VIII

1. Robert Archey Woods, *English Social Movements* (London: Swan, Sonnenschein & Co., 1892), pp. 24-25.

2. Lillian A. Covell (trans.), *Toynbee Hall and the English Settlement Movement*, by Dr. Werner Picht (London: Salvationist Publishing and Supplies, Ltd., N.D.), p. 50.

3. Woods, *English Social Movements*, p. 80.

4. Covell, *Toynbee Hall*, p. 95.

5. Mrs. Humphry Ward, *University Hall: Opening Address* (London: Smith, Elder, & Co., 1891), p. 13.

6. Ibid., p. 43.

7. Ibid., pp. 38-39.

8. Two University Men (eds.), *Modern Evangelistic Movements* (London: Thomson & Cowan, 1924), p. 52.

9. Woods, *Eng. Soc. Movements*, p. 103.

10. Ibid., pp. 106-07.

11. Ibid., p. 102.

12. Ibid., pp. 96-97.

13. Inglis, *Churches and Working Classes*, p. 156.

14. Haw, *Christianity and Working Classes*, p. 59.

15. Ibid., pp. 60-61.

16. Men, *Mod. Evang. Movements*, p. 54.

17. Ibid., p. 56.

18. Ibid., p. 57.

19. Inglis, *Churches and Working Classes*, p. 144.

20. Ibid., p. 155.

21. Covell, *Toynbee Hall*, pp. 1-2.

22. Woods, *Eng. Soc. Movements*, p. 117.

23. Men, *Mod. Evang. Movements*, pp. 57-58.

24. Covell, *Toynbee Hall*, pp. 126-127.

25. Ibid., p. 129.

26. Rev. W. H. Rooper, *General Booth and the Salvation Army*

(London: Simpkin, Marshall, Hamilton, Kent, & Co., Limited, 1892), p. 5.

27. Covell, *Toynbee Hall*, pp. 130-131.

28. Ibid., p. 132.

29. Ibid., p. 130.

30. Ibid.

31. Ibid., p. 136.

32. Inglis, *Churches and Working Classes*, p. 175.

33. "Go in the Power of the Holy Ghost," *All The World*, I, 2(December 1884), 14.

34. Railton, *General Booth*, p. 11.

35. Bramwell Booth, "Addresses," p. 70.

36. Ibid., p. 104.

37. *Doctrines of S.A.*, 39.

38. Bramwell Booth, "Addresses," pp. 71-72.

39. Railton, *General Booth*, p. 125.

40. *International Young People's Company Orders for 1906* (London: 79-81, Fortress Road, N.W., 1905), p. vi.

41. *International Young People's Company Orders for 1905* (London: 79-81, Fortress Road, N.W., 1904), p. vi.

42. Ibid., p. xiii.

43. *Truth, Religious Persecution. Sleeping Christianity. An Answer to "Behind the Scenes with the Salvation Army"* (London: Civil Service Printing and Publishing Company, Limited, 8, Salisbury Court, Fleet Street, E.C., July 19, 1882), p. 16.

44. Ibid.

45. Railton, *General Booth*, p. 126.

46. Orders for 1906, p. xiii.

47. Railton, *General Booth*, p. 126.

48. *Orders for 1906*, p. xiii.

49. Ibid.

50. Major Miles, "Junior Cadet Brigade," *The Officer*, II, 6(June 1894), 172.

51. *The Coming Army* (London: International Headquarters, 101, Queen Victoria Street, c. 1888), p. 10.

52. *A School of the Prophets: A Sketch of Training Home Life* (2d ed.; London: The Salvation Army Book Department, 1901), pp. 3-4.

53. Railton, *General Booth*, p. 145.

54. Railton, *Heathen England*, pp. 122-123.

55. Ibid., p. 116.

56. J. O. Bairstow, *Sensational Religion, in Past and the Present Day* (London: Elliot Stock, 62, Paternoster Row, E.C., 1890), p. 56.

57. The General, *Talks with Officers*, p. 1.

58. Railton, *General Booth*, p. 77.

59. Ibid.

60. William Booth, "Our New Name," *The Salvationist*, XI (January 1, 1879), 2.

61. Railton, *General Booth*, p. 59.

62. The General, "A Fair Wind for Salvation," *The Officer*, I, 4(April 1893), 99.

63. Mrs. Booth, "Compel Them to Come In," *The East London Evangelist*, I (March 1, 1869), 84.

64. Railton, *General Booth*, p. 153.

65. "America," *All The World*, I, 3(January 1885), 32.

66. Ibid.

67. The General, *Talks with Officers*, p. 14.

68. "News Notes," *The Officer*, I, 4(April 1893), 107.

69. The General, *Talks with Officers*, p. 14.

70. S., W.B., *A Letter To William Booth, The "General" of the, So-Called, "Salvation Army"* (London: Cockhead, 94, Norfolk Terrace, Bayswater, 1882), pp. 4-5.

71. C. Raleigh Chichester, "The Salvation Army," *The Month: A Catholic Magazine and Review*, XLIV, 214(April 1882), 480.

72. The General, *Talks with Officers*, p. 5.

73. Ibid., p. 4.

74. Bramwell Booth, "Addresses," p. 8.

75. O.W.L.A., *Some Reasons Why*, pp. 20-21.

76. John Bascom, *The New Theology* (London: G. P. Putnam's Sons, 1891), p. 471.

77. Charles T. Pratt, *The Salvation Army: A Sermon Preached in Hawthorne Church* (Barnsley: I. W. Davis, Printer and Bookseller, 16, Market Hill, 1882), p. 7.

78. Ibid., pp. 8-9.

79. O.W.L.A., *Some Reasons Why*, p. 17.

80. Bramwell Booth, "Addresses," p. 144.

81. "Sociology. The Lord's Prayer in Eight Vollies," *The War Cry*, 735, (August 30, 1890), p. 4.

82. Ibid.

Chapter X

1. Walter J. Ong, *The Presence of the Word* (New York: Simon and Schuster [A Clarion Book], 1967), p. 54.

2. Ibid., p. 32.

3. Ibid., pp. 44-45.

4. W. Hastie, *Theology as Science* (Glasgow: James MacLehose and Sons, 1899), p. 8.

5. Ibid.

6. Ong, *Presence*, p. 40.

7. Thomas Carlyle, "Signs of the Times," *Sartor Resartus and Selected Prose*, intro. Herbert Sussman (New York: Holt, Rinehart and Winston, 1970), p. 16.

8. Ibid.

9. Ibid., p. 27.

10. John Stuart Mill, "Utilitarianism," *The Utilitarians* (Garden City, New York: Anchor Books, 1973), pp. 406-412.

11. Thomas Carlyle, "Past and Present," *Sartor Resartus and Selected Prose*, intro. Herbert Sussman (New York: Holt, Rinehart and Winston, 1970), p. 284.

12. Bairstow, *Sensational Religion*, p. 51.

13. Dr. William M. Taylor, "Sensationalism in the Pulpit," *The Primitive Methodist Quarterly*, I (April 1879), 327-328.

14. Ibid., p. 328.

15. Ibid., p. 330.

16. Ibid., p. 333.

17. O.W.L.A., *Some Reasons Why*, p. 15.

18. Ibid., p. 13.

19. "Leading Article on S.A. and its Right to Procession," *The Times* [London], June 14, 1882, p. 9.

20. The Editor, "The Salvation Army and Darkest England," *The Month*, LXX (September - December, 1890), 471.

21. "Art. VI. - The Salvation Army," *The Church Quarterly Review*, XIV (April 1882), 117.

22. John Price, *The Salvation Army Tested by their Works* (Chester: Minshull and Hughes, Eastgate Row, 1882), pp. 10-11.

23. Truth, *Religious Persecution*, pp. 6-7.

24. Ibid., p. 7.

25. Price, *Salvation Army Tested*, p. 21.

26. "Art. XI - Darkest England," *The Church Quarterly Review*, XXXII (April 4, 1891), p. 246.

27. The Editor, "The Salvation Army and Darkest England," *The Month*, LXX (September - December, 1890), 470.

28. "The Salvation Army In Geneva," *The Times* [London], February 21, 1883, p. 12.

29. Ibid.

30. Bramwell Booth, *These Fifty Years* (London: Cassell & Company Ltd., 1929), pp. 23-24.

31. Dr. William M. Taylor, "Sensationalism in the Pulpit," *The Primitive Methodist Quarterly Review*, I (April, 1879), 327.

32. *Sensation or Salvation?* (London: Civil Service Printing and Publishing Company, Limited, 8, Salisbury Court, Fleet Street, E.C., 1882), p. 4.

33. Haw, *Christianity and Working Classes*, p. 48.

34. Ibid., p. 49.

35. Ibid., p. 50.

36. Ibid.

37. Ibid., p. 99.

38. Ibid., p. 55.

Chapter XI

1. *International Young People's Company Orders for 1909* (London: 79-81, Fortress Road, N.W., 1908), pp. xii-xvi.

2. *International Young People's Company Orders for 1911* (London: 79-81, Fortress Road, N.W., 1910), p. xii.

3. "Closet Prayer," *The East London Evangelist* I (May 1, 1869), 117.

4. "The Claims of Our Large Towns on the Churches," *The Wesleyan-Methodist Magazine*, I (June, 1877), 450-51.

5. "Incidents and Illustrations," *The Officer*, II, 5(May, 1894), 158.

6. "Subject Notes," *The Officer*, II, 3(March 1894), 87-88.

7. Inglis, *Churches and Working Classes*, p. 176.

8. W. Corbridge, *Salvation Mine* (London: Salvation Army Stores, 101, Queen Victoria Street, E.C., 1881), p. 2.

9. The Editor, "My Last Year on Earth," *The Officer*, II, 1(January, 1884), 4.

10. Covell, *Toynbee Hall*, p. 119.

11. Woods, *English Social Movements*, pp. 86-87.

12. Charles B. Waller, *The Salvation Army: How should The Thoughtful Christian Judge This Movement?* (London: Kegan Paul, Trench, & Co., 1 Paternoster Square, 1882), 7-8.

13. Alfred G. Cunningham and Wm. Booth, *The Bible: Its Divine Revelation, Inspiration and Authority* (London: Salvationists Publishing and Supplies, Ltd., 1961), p. 14.

14. Ibid., p. 13.

15. *Doctrines of S.A.*, p. 109.

16. *International Young People's Company Orders for 1907* (London: 79-81, Fortress Road, N.W., 1906), p. ix.

17. Ibid.

18. Ibid., p. xi-xii.

19. Ibid., p. xi.

20. Ibid.

21. *School of Prophets,* pp. 67-68.

22. Mrs. Booth, "The Kingdom of Christ," *All The World,* I, 10(August 1885), 183.

23. Ibid.

24. Bramwell Booth, "Addresses," p. 63.

25. Blackfriars (trans.), *Summa Theologiae,* by Thomas Aquinas, I (New York: McGraw-Hill Book Company, 1963), 1a, 3, 1.

26. Ibid., 1a, 1, 10, Reply to Obj. 1.

27. Thomas Gilby (trans.), *St. Thomas Aquinas Theological Texts* (London: Oxford University Press, 1955), p. 18.

28. J. Van Der Ploeg, "The Place of Holy Scripture in the Theology of St. Thomas," *The Tomist,* X (1947), 417-422.

29. Gilby, *St. Thomas,* p. 18.

30. The English Dominican Fathers (trans.), *The Summa Contra Gentiles IV,* by St. Thomas Aquinas (London: Burns Oates & Washbourne Ltd., 1929), p. 121.

31. Heasman, *Evangelicals in Action,* p. 16.

32. *Orders for 1906,* p. 5.

33. Bramwell Booth, "Addresses," p. 61.

34. Cunningham, *The Bible,* p. 13.

35. Mrs. Booth, "Heart Backsliding," *The East London Evangelist,* I (April 1869), 97.

36. *Doctrines of S.A.,* p. 15.

37. The General, "A Ghost Story," *The Officer,* II, 5(May, 1894), 129.

38. Mrs. Booth, "The Kingdom of Christ," p. 183.

39. Ibid., p. 184.

40. Bramwell Booth, "Addresses," p. 10.

41. "India," *All The World,* I (November 1894), 5.

42. *Doctrines of S.A.,* p. 118.

43. F. G. Jannaway, *The Salvation Army and the Bible*

(Birmingham: C. C. Walker, 21, Hendon Road, Sparkhill, 1909), p. 5.

44. Ibid., p. 8.

45. *Doctrines of S.A.*, p. 111.

46. O.W.L.A., *Some Reasons Why,* p. 18.

47. Ibid., p. 20.

48. Truth, *Religious Persecution,* p. 10.

49. Ibid.

50. Price, *Salvation Army Tested,* p. 5.

51. Ibid.

52. Bairstow, *Sensational Religion,* pp. 6-7.

53. "Invasion of U.S.," *The War Cry,* 9, February 21, 1880, p. 1

54. Men, *Mod. Evang. Movements,* p. 24.

55. "The Salvation Army," *The Times* [London], April 19, 1881, p. 5.

56. William Booth, "Our New Name," *The Salvationists,* XI (January 1, 1879), 1.

57. Commissioner Railton, "Easter In Hell," *The Officer,* I, 3(March, 1893), 75.

58. Bramwell Booth, *These Fifty Years* (London:Cassell & Company Ltd., 1929), p. 14.

59. Ibid., p. 15.

60. Minnie L. Carpenter, *Commissioner John Lawley* (London: Salvationists Publishing and Supplies, Ltd, 1924), pp. 7-8.

61. Ibid., p. 131.

62. The General, "The Salvation Army," *The Salvationists,* XI (February 1, 1879), 29.

63. Bairstow, *Sensational Religion,* p. 27.

64. Railton, *General Booth,* p. 68.

65. "Go in the Power of the Holy Ghost," *All The World,* I, 2(December, 1884), 13.

Chapter XII

1. Ong, *Presence*, p. 30.

2. "Ratcliffe Highway," *The East London Evangelist*, I (March 1, 1869), 90-91.

3. Railton, *Heathen England*, p. 129.

4. Ibid., p. 153.

5. Bramwell Booth, *These Fifty Years*, p. 84.

6. R. J. Evans, *The Victorian Age 1815-1914* (2d ed.; London: Edward Arnold, 1968), p. 279.

7. *Opinions of Eminent Persons*, p. 41.

8. Watson Smith, "Darkest England Scheme," *The Darkest England Gazette*, 4(July 22, 1893), p. 5.

9. Haw, *Christianity and Working Classes*, pp. 155-56.

10. "Opportunity and Responsibility," *The Officer*, II, 6(June, 1894), 166.

11. Inglis, *Churches and Working Classes*, p. 35.

12. Ibid., p. 45.

13. Ibid.

14. Railton, *General Booth*, p. 17.

15. Truth, *Religious Persecution*, p. 5.

16. Heathcote, *My Army Experience*, p. 27.

17. Ibid.

18. Ibid., p. 28.

19. Ibid.

20. *Opinions of Eminent Persons*, p. 32.

21. *The Wesleyan Spectator and General Review of Religion, Literature, and Social Economy*, Vol. I (London: John Wiley, 73, Fleet Street, 1863), p. 183.

22. Ibid.

23. Ibid.

24. Bairstow, *Sensational Religion*, p. 66.

25. Thomas Lawrence, "The Salvation Army," *The Primitive*

Methodist Quarterly Review, IV (April, 1882), 293.

26. *Sensation or Salvation,* p. 5.

27. The Editor, "The Salvation Army and Darkest England," *The Month,* LXX (September - December, 1890), 473.

28. Bairstow, *Sensational Religion,* p. 3.

29. Railton, *Heathen England,* p. 185.

30. R. I. L., "Wear Your Uniform," *The War Cry,* No. 721 (May 24, 1890), p. 2.

31. "Leading Article," *The Times* [London], October 13, 1881, p. 9.

32. "The 'Salvation Army' in South London," *The Times* [London], October 22, 1879, p. 9.

33. Chichester, "The Salvation Army," *The Month,* p. 482.

34. William Booth, "How to Manage A Mission Station," *The Christian Mission Magazine,* VIII (July, 1876), 153.

35. Men, *Mod. Evang. Movements,* p. 27

36. Ibid., p. 28.

37. "Violent Religion," *The Christian Mission Magazine* VIII (September, 1876), 211.

38. Railton, *Heathen England,* p. 62.

39. Ibid.

40. William Booth, *A Talk With Mr. Gladstone at His Own Fireside: By General Booth* (London: Simpkin, Marshall, Hamilton, Kent & Co., Limited, 1897), p. 34.

41. Truth, *Religious Persecution,* p. 14.

42. "The Salvation Army," *The Times* [London], May 30, 1882, p. 4.

43. Inglis, *Churches and Working Classes,* pp. 187-88.

44. "Art. VI. - The Salvation Army," *The Church Quarterly Review,* XIV (April 1882), 117.

45. William Booth, *Talk With Gladstone,* p. 26.

46. *Sensation or Salvation,* p. 6.

47. Waller, *The Salvation Army: How Should,* p. 10.

48. *Sensation or Salvation,* p. 6.

49. The General, *Talks With Officers,* p. 11.

50. The Editor, "The Salvation Army and Darkest England," *The Month,* LXX (September - December, 1890), 469-470.

51. Ibid., p. 471.

52. Ibid., p. 472.

53. Ibid.

54. "How To Succeed," *The Officer,* II, 4(April, 1894), 100.

55. *Doctrines of S.A.,* p. 6.

56. Ibid., p. 7.

57. Ibid., p. 13.

58. Ibid., p. 78.

59. Railton, *Heathen England,* p. 34.

60. "Go," *All The World,* I, 1(November, 1884), 4.

61. Chichester, "The Salvation Army," *The Month,* p. 474.

62"United States," *All The World,* I, 7(May, 1885), 122.

63. E. Swift Brengle, "Why Am I A Salvationist?", *All The World,* VI, 8(August, 1890), 363.

64. Ibid.

65. "An Atheist on the Salvation Army," *All The World,* I, 9(July, 1885), 163.

66. "Go in the Power of the Holy Ghost," *All The World,* I, 2(December, 1884), 13.

67. "Human Nature," *The Officer,* II, 7(July, 1884), 223.

68. Railton, *General Booth,* p. 70.

69. William Booth, "How to Manage A Mission Station," *The Christian Mission Magazine,* VIII (July, 1876), 149.

70. General Booth, "Addresses," p. 114.

71. "The Salvation Army In Geneva," *The Times* [London], February 21, 1883, p. 12.

72. "The Salvation Army In Geneva," *The Times* [London], February 24, 1883, p. 8.

73. Frank Smith, "Sociology. The Lord's Prayer in Eight Vollies," *The War Cry,* 737 (September 13, 1890), p. 6.

74. Carpenter, *Lawley,* p. 66.

Chapter XIII

1. "Hackney," *The Christian Mission Magazine*, VIII (February, 1876), 40.

2. Railton, *Heathen England*, p. 29.

3. William Booth, "To My Officers," *The Officer*, I, 1(January, 1893), 2.

4. Ibid.

5. Carpenter, *Lawley*, pp. 107-108.

6. Ibid., p. 108.

7. "Our Paper War," *The Officer*, I, 1(January, 1893), 4.

8. The Editor, "Editor's Chat," *The Officer*, I, 2(February, 1893), 48.

9. Jesse Page, *General Booth: The Man And His Work* (London: S. W. Partridge & Co., 1901), pp. 46-47.

10. Ibid., p. 48.

11. "Invasion of U.S.," *The War Cry*, 9, (February 21, 1880), p. 1.

12. The General, "The Millenium; or The Ultimate Triumph of Salvation Army Principles," *All The World*, VI, 8(August, 1890), 338.

13. Ibid., p. 337.

14. "The 'Salvation Army,'" *The Times* [London], September 20, 1881, p. 8.

15. *Spiritual Conflict: A Glance at the Every Day Work of The Salvation Army* (London: 101, Queen Victoria Street, E.C., 1902), p. 9.

16. "Our Foreign Field," *The Officer*, I, 2(February, 1893), 46.

17. The General, *Talks With Officers*, p. 3.

18. Bramwell Booth, "Addresses," pp. 2-3.

19. S., W.B., *A Letter to William Booth*, p. 4.

20. Truth, *Religious Persecution*, p. 9.

21. T. H. Huxley, *Social Diseases and Worse Remedies* (London: Macmillan and Co., 1891), p. 58.

22. Inglis, *Churches And Working Classes*, p. 208.

23. S., A., *The New Papacy: Behind the Scenes* (Toronto: Albert Britness, 1889), p. 7.

24. Pope Booth, *The Salvation Army*, A.D. 1950, (London: W. Lucas, 42 and 43, Essex-Street, 1890), p. 4.

25. "A Story of Twelve Month's Work," *The Christian Mission Magazine*, VIII (March, 1876), 49.

26. Ibid.

27. George Railton, "On," *The Christian Mission Magazine*, VIII (January, 1876), 4.

28. Truth, *Religious Persecution*, p. 8.

29. Waller, *The Salvation Army*, p. 11.

30. Ibid., p. 12.

31. Railton, *Heathen England*, p. 134.

32. E. O. B. (trans), *Read and Judge The (So-Called), Salvation Army*, by La Comtesse Agenor de Gasparin (London: Griffith & Farran, 1883), p. 30.

33. Bramwell Booth, "Addresses," p. 99.

34. Bramwell Booth, *These Fifty Years*, p. 98.

35. S. A. Blackwood and others, "The Salvation Army," *The Salvationist*, XI (February 1, 1879), 35.

36. Bairstow, *Sensational Religion*, pp. 55-56.

37. The General, "The General on Leadership," *The Officer*, II, 7(July 1894), 195-96.

38. Albert Muspratt, *The Salvation Army: Is It A Benefit to the Cause of Religion* (Ripon: Printed and Published by William Harrison, Market Place, 1884), p. 6.

39. Haw, *Christianity And Working Classes*, pp. 40-41.

40. The General, "The General on First Principles and Dangers," *The Officer*, I, 1(January, 1893), 12.

41. Ibid.

42. Inglis, *Churches And Working Classes*, p. 178.

43. "The East London Christian Mission," *The East London Evangelist*, I (October, 1868), 3.

44. "To My Officers," *The Officer*, I, 1(January, 1893), 1.

45. The General, "First Principles," *The Officer*, p. 12.

46. Ibid.

47. "To My Officers," *The Officer*, p. 2.

48. The General, "In Darkest England and The Way Out," *The War Cry*, November 15, 1890, p. 9.

49. Heathcote, *Army Experience*, pp. 18-19.

50. "The General on Leadership," *The Officer*, II, 7(July, 1894), 196.

51. Truth, *Religious Persecution*, p. 4.

52. Carpenter, *Lawley*, p. 25.

53. Ibid., p. 82.

54. Ibid., pp. 82-83.

55. "Consett: A Night With The Hallelujah Army," *The Salvationist*, XI (January 1, 1879), 8.

56. Bramwell Booth, *Essays and Sketches*, p. 42.

57. Ibid.

58. Railton, *General Booth*, p. 91.

59. "The Salvation Army," *The Times* [London], May 26, 1880, p. 7.

60. Ford C. Ottman, *Herbert Booth* (New York: Doubleday, Doran & Company, Inc., 1928), p. 285.

61. Ibid., p. 286.

62. Thomas Lawrence, "The Salvation Army," *The Primitive Methodist Quarterly Review*, IV (April, 1882), 296.

63. Heathcote, *Army Experience*, p. 23.

64. Ibid., p. 59.

65. Ibid., p. 23.

66. "Three Words To Officers," *The Officer*, I, 2(February, 1893), 41.

67. Ibid.

68. Ibid.

69. Ibid.

70. Ibid.

71. Ibid.

72. Roland Robertson, "The Salvation Army: the Persistence of Sectarianism," *Patterns of Sectarianism: Organisation and Ideology in Social and Religious Movements* (London: Heinemann, 1967), p. 78.

73. Inglis, *Churches and Working Classes*, p. 213.

74. Bramwell Booth, "Addresses," pp. 3-4.

75. Railton, *General Booth*, p. 102.

Vita

John Rosario Rhemick

Birth: August 1, 1939, Rome, New York.

Colleges Attended:
Valley Forge Military Academy Junior College
Utica College of Syracuse University
New York State University at Buffalo
Columbia University
Asbury College
Asbury Theological Seminary
Northwestern University—Garrett-Evangelical Theological
Seminary

Degrees Earned:
B.A., Asbury College, 1971.
M.Div., Asbury Theological Seminary, 1973.
M.A., Northwestern University, 1975.
Ph.D., Northwestern University, 1984.